# SPAIN TODAY

## ESSAYS ON LITERATURE, CULTURE, SOCIETY

*Edited by*

José Colmeiro,
Christina Dupláa,
Patricia Greene,
Juana Sabadell

Dartmouth College
Dept. of Spanish and Portuguese
1995

Published by
Dartmouth College (Hanover, New Hampshire)
Department of Spanish and Portuguese.



ISBN 0-9648929-0-1



Copies of this book can be purchased by individuals ($15.00) and institutions ($25.00) by check or money order payable to Dartmouth College from:

Anne Weatherman
Dept of Spanish and Portuguese
6072 Dartmouth Hall
Dartmouth College
Hanover, NH 03755-3511
Tel. (603) 646-1462
FAX (603) 646-3695

This conference was made possible thanks to the support of the Fundació 'la Caixa' (Barcelona), The Dickey Center for International Understanding, the Fundación Isaac Albéniz, the General Consulate of Spain (Boston), the Office of the Dean of the Faculty, and the Dept. of Spanish and Portuguese.

The editors would like to thank the invaluable assistance of Anne Weatherman from the Dept. of Spanish, Otmar Foelsche and Susan Bibeau from Humanities Computing, and Martin Sherwin, Director of the Dickey Center.

Cover artwork: "Flor 9 (triptic)", by José María Sicilia
Fundació 'la Caixa" (Barcelona)

# SPAIN TODAY
# ESSAYS ON LITERATURE, CULTURE, SOCIETY

## Introduction

José Colmeiro, Christina Dupláa,
Patricia Greene and Juana Sabadell

This collection of critical essays is the result of the international symposium "**Spain Today: Literature, Culture, Society**" which took place on November 10-12, 1994 at Dartmouth College. The purpose of the symposium was to present an interdisciplinary reassessment of the contemporary cultural forces and critical currents that have completely redefined Spain in the last two decades. The cultural renaissance that has taken shape in Spain following the political transition from dictatorship to democracy has manifested itself in a variety of forms: the recovery and normalization of a strong and plural diversity, the expansion of mass media technologies, the commodification of cultural production, the consolidation of public and private institutions, and the demarginalization of discourses marked by gender, class and ethnicity. The papers presented at the symposium by scholars from both sides of the Atlantic addressed the impact of this cultural renovation from new critical perspectives within the framework of Neo-Hispanism, and reflected the diversity and plurality of currents in the field of contemporary Iberian Studies.

This conference represents the first exploration in the United States of the concept of Neo-Hispanism, understood as a specific field of inquiry within an interdisciplinary critical approach encompassing the plurality of manifestations of hispanic culture and, more particularlly for Iberian Studies, the multicultural and multilingual realities of Spain. The notion of Neo-Hispanism was first discussed at the encounter of scholars from Europe and the United States "Catalunya en el extranjero" (Barcelona, November 30-December 1, 1993), and was followed up by a special session at the MLA convention devoted to this topic: "Neo-Hispanism: Towards a Concept of Pluralism" (San Diego, December 1994). The impact of this project has already been felt in academia throughout campuses nationwide in terms of other scholarly encounters and curricular innovations.

Parallel events in conjunction with the "Spain Today" symposium, included book exhibits on contemporary Spanish literature, film, culture and critical therory, and the ten-week Film Series of contemporary Spanish cinema entitled "Screening

Spain Today". The Spanish films from the 1990s presented in this series included ¡Ay, Carmela!, Jamón Jamón, Cómo ser mujer y no morir en el intento, Jardines Colgantes, Kika, Belle Epoque, Intruso, and El sol del membrillo. In addition, a series of roundtable discussions were held on "Spanish Culture and Society Towards a New Century" and "The Politics of Culture: Private and Public Institutions" with the participation of representatives from major cultural foundations and governmental institutions: Antoni Millet (Fundació "la Caixa"), Vicente Ferrer (Fundación Isaac Albéniz), José María Conget (Instituto Cervantes) and Darío Villanueva (Universidade de Santiago de Compostela). Closing remarks were offered by Carlos Saenz de Boado (General Consul of Spain, Boston) and Martin J. Sherwin (The Dickey Center).

The opening essay of **Spain Today. Essays on Literature, Culture, Society** by well-known Spanish author Lourdes Ortiz poses the question *¿Qué puede la literatura?* This inspiring essay attempts to define the role of literature in a contemporary cultural context that has undergone drastic changes in recent decades. Ortiz' declaration challenges us as readers and critics to think about the power of the written word (its limitations as well as its extraordinary possibilities) as we read this collection of essays.

The section of the book entitled **Literature and History: New Critical Perspectives** is devoted to the reevaluation of the relationship between historical and literary discourses in 20th century Spain. Victor Fuentes presents in his essay "More Than Three Forms of Distortion in 20th Century Spanish Literary Historiography: Counterpoint Alternatives" an insightful critique of the limitations and omissions in the canons of contemporary Spanish literary historiography. Fuentes delineates an alternative model for a possible history of modern Spanish literarature, a model based on discontinuity, plurality, division, differences and resistances, underlining the conflictive nature of literary and social realities in modern Spain. Fuentes criticizes the ahistorical character of Spanish literary histories and their reliance on the worn out model of the "generation" concept, which displaces the issues of class, gender, and ethnicity. Instead, Fuentes advocates the recovery of repressed, silenced or marginalized genealogies in Spanish literary histories. He highlights the silencing of the social and popular literature starting in the 1920s and 1930s and the relegation of the Spanish literature produced in exile. Fuentes also underlines the mutual interrelationship of Spanish and Spanish American literatures (Vallejo, Valle Inclán, Sender), and the need to create a new history enriched by the diverse national cultures other that Castilian.

David K. Herzberger in his compelling essay "Reading Fiction through Historiography (or Vice Versa?)" addresses the intertextuality of historiographical and literary texts in the context of Spain's recent past, arguing that we must engage historiography through fiction -and vice versa- for a complete understanding of that past. Herzberger points out that since New Historicist approaches have promoted the dissolution of traditional barriers between discourses, the juxtaposition of historiography and fiction creates an intertextual defamiliarization, changing the signifying codes of each, and opening them to reinterpretation. Herzberger argues that the Francoist historiographers' reappropriation of history was achieved by means of intertextual connections with other sacralized texts, most notably those by Menéndez y Pelayo. Through this reappropriation, the master narrative of Francoist historiography presents a universalist perspective of the Spanish past, devoid of contingency and ambiguity and based on a single monolithic truth which absorbs diversity and dissallows differences. Herzberger points out the diversity of literary counterdiscourses written under and after Franco which reacted against this monological discourse embodying a single historical vision, but he focuses particularly on the postmodern fiction of Torrente Ballester written after 1975. For Herberger, Torrente Ballester's works clearly insist on the discursive core of history and fiction, whose referents are always other discourses, opening up new ways of intertextual dissidence against Francoist historiography. Herzberger argues convincingly that Torrente Ballester's postmodern fiction, characterized by the disintegration of a unified voice, where traditional notions of realist representation and referentiality are questioned and final truths are dispersed, sustains difference and contradiction instead of erasing them.

The section devoted to contemporary Spanish cinema **Spain on Screen** offers new critical approaches exploring the present process of reformulation of Spanish cinematic culture. These groundbreaking essays, informed by the current debates in cultural theory, multiculturalism, gender studies, and postmodern theory, analyze the reconfiguration of Spanish cinema and its creative responses to the national and transnational challenges to its identity. The authors of these essays explore alternative ways of imagining Spain on the screen in the 1990's and attest to the creation of a new Spanish cinematic culture.

Jaume Martí-Olivella's essay "Towards a New Transcultural Dialogue in Spanish Film" is firmly grounded on the need to reconceptualize the notions of nationalism and feminism in contemporary Spanish culture, advocating the construction of a multicultural, heteroglossic and plurinational space, an "imagined community" that might still be called Spain. The dream language of cinematic images is particularly appropriate for this purpose, Martí-Olivella convincingly argues, since it permits to (re)create a transcultural dialogue based on the (re)construction of both individual and national identities, where the personal past has a political importance for the collective. Martí-Olivella discusses two particular examples of gendered film discourses which establish the visual foundation for a new dialogue across Spain's different languages and cultures: Arantxa Lazcano's film in Basque Urte Ilunak (The Dark Years) and Pilar Miró's El pájaro de la felicidad (The Bird of Happiness) in Catalan and Castilian. By sliding the signifiers of center and margin, presenting the marginal and marked as "regional" in national non-marginal contexts, in these films the marginal becomes normalized, producing a new alternative in the process of recognition of Spain's multicultural reality.

Marvin D'Lugo in his essay "Bigas Luna's Jamón Jamón: Remaking the National in Spanish Cinema" lucidly sketches the problematics of the current refiguration of Spanish cinema, struggling against the challenges to traditional notions of national cinemas and the globalization of media technologies. With the postmodern commodification of culture, the self-concious commercial performance of the auteur has offered a creative response to the crisis of national cinema. D'Lugo claims that the new Spanish authorial cinema exemplified in Bigas Luna's Jamón Jamón has provided symptomatic responses to the crisis of national culture and commerce, reaching an international audience through a reformulation of the notion of Spain and the commercial exploitation of images coded as "Spanish". D'Lugo coincides with Smith's take on Almodóvar, arguing that Jamón Jamón is as much a response to as a symptom of the crisis of contemporary cinematic cultures, but he questions its characterization as an Almodóvar spin-off. According to D'Lugo, Jamón Jamón brings to a transnational audience caricatures of archaic symbols of stereotypical Spanishness (masculinity, sensuality) while it allows Spanish audiences to reflect upon their own self-image and essence. D'Lugo sees Jamón Jamón as a self-referential interrogation of the traditional constructions of Spain, the practices and images of Spanish popular culture, subject to perpetual reformulations of comodification and commercialization. Bigas Luna's "retratos ibéricos" offer a picture of Spanish culture in the process of refiguring itself as a postmodern commodified culture.

Paul Julian Smith's essay problematizes Pedro Almodóvar's Kika (1993) in light of current cultural theory focused on the technologies of visual representation. Smith bases his analysis on Paul Virilio's concept of the "vision machine", a form of sightless vision and automated perception which overemphasizes visibility but paradoxically produces a waning of reality. Smith persuasively argues that this logic is the basis of the constant con/fusion of presentation and representation in Kika, directly related to the decline of cinema and the rise of video. Understanding Almodóvar's film as a critique of reproductive visual technology in the video era of instant duplication, Smith considers the film both a comment and a symptom of the depersonalitation of vision and duplication of the body which follows in the wake of the vision machine. In this respect, Kika displays the depersonalized and delocalized perception typical of the phatic image which prizes intensity and immediacy.

The three essays included in the section **Feminist Discourses: Reclaiming Subjectivities** represent new ways of re/reading the literary and historical canon of modern Spain from feminist perspectives. Susan Kirkpatrick's essay explores how certain mysoginist discourses have denigrated --through the feminization of language-- new threatening forms of cultural production. Cristina Enríquez de Salamanca traces the construction of the political subject and the ensuing approval of universal suffrage in 1932 to the Virtuous Domestic Woman of the nineteenth century. Geraldine Nichols brings to the center

Catalan women's marginal discourses informed by nationalism, class and gender.

Susan Kirkpatrick's lucid study "Gender and Difference in *Fin de siglo* Literary Discourse" is a reflection on how gender difference and gender confusion become key tropes in discourses about nineteenth-century Spanish culture and society. Kirkpatrick suggests that discourses of gender difference linked denigrating images of femininity (perverse, pathological, weak-minded, deformed and degenerate) to the supposed degeneration and decadence that was overtaking Western Europe. As Kirkpatrick illustrates, these tropes pervaded discussions from the positivist social sciences to literary and aesthetic arguments about national identity. According to Kirkpartrick, writers such as *Clarín* (Su único hijo) and Galdos's (Tristana) showed a preoccupation with those discourses and practices that threatened to erase the difference between genders; while others like Emilia Pardo Bazán reaffirmed their beliefs regarding women's parity to men. Interestingly, Kirkpatrick observes that in the aftermath of the Spanish defeat of 1898, the rhetoric linking the feminine with the decadent would increase in intensity; at the same time, literary critics and historians would carefully construct a narrative that would distinguish the virile and energetic Generation of 1898 from the degenerate and feminized Latin American *modernistas*. Susan Kirkpatrick concludes her insightful essay by invoking the new, dissonant voices of turn-of-the-century Spanish feminist discourse which challenged the abjection of feminine difference while resisting the role of idealized femininity as represented by the *ángel del hogar*

Cristina Enríquez de Salamanca's innovative study "The Question of the Political Subject in Nineteeth-Century Spanish Domestic Discourse" problematizes the two conflicting models of female subjectivity proposed by scholars of nineteenth-century Spanish culture. Enríquez de Salamanca argues that the granting of women's suffrage in the 1932 Republican Constitution was paradoxically grounded in the model of "difference" rather than the model of "equality". She posits that through the image of a Virtuous Domestic Woman who was also a writing subject, nineteenth-century female domestic writers made possible the concept of an imagined female community within the public sphere, thus bringing middle class women into the social and political arena. By revising what Spanish society considered to be "natural" to women, nineteenth-century domestic writing became the basis for the construction of a separate political consciousness culminating in the granting of political recognition by the Spanish Second Republic.

Geraldine Nichols's perceptive essay "The Construction of Subjectivity in Contemporary Women Writers of Catalonia" explores how such fundamental categories as nationalism, class and gender have shaped the complex subjectivity of contemporary Catalan writers Ana María Moix, Montserrat Roig and Carme Riera. Nichols finds particularly useful for her analysis the concept of identity as a matrix of subject positions since Moix, Roig, and Riera continually negotiate their identities through diverse and often contradictory messages regarding their class origin, religion, sexuality, and nationalist politics. Nichols suggests that Moix, Roig and Riera write from a "fractured subjectivity" since they are relegated to the position of insiders/outsiders insofar as they write about the selvage, rather than about the cloth itself, in essence creating an alternative discourse which encourages new forms of subjectivity. Nichols illustrates how these conflicting subjectivities are constructed through a series of metaphors such as the selvage, the cracked plate or the fractured mirror. Moreover, Nichols examines how these fragile and complex identities are projected without shattering onto literature and how they are reflected in the content and form of that literature. Geraldine Nichols concludes that regardless of the metaphors chosen to represent the fractured subjectivity present in the fiction of Moix, Roig and Riera, all three authors resist being inscribed by silence. Instead Ana María Moix, Montserrat Roig and Carme Riera claim that the voice heard from the margins deserves a place in discourse.

The last section of the book, **Looking Ahead in Iberian Studies**, presents an analysis of the ongoing trends in Neo-Hispanim and a discussion of the alternative scholarly approaches for the future. Dionisio Cañas's essay argues that a mixture of existential disbelief and creative enthusiasm is reshaping, to a certain extent, the postmodern subject in general, and more specifically the poetic subject of the 21st century. Cañas claims that the alliance between technology and imagination, individual and society, and originality and collectivism will play a central part in this subjective transformation, and that the material bases, the media, and the literary and artistic genres will necessarily be altered and enriched. He situates the future of Spanish poetry in the revalorization of its poetic imagination in conjunction with new stimuli and new technologies; in other words, he envisions a poetic language moving along with a dynamic social context. This is the kind of imagination that he believes to be absent from most contemporary poetic practices. In his analysis of the current state of Spanish poetry, Cañas reviews the anthologies and the efforts that have marked post-modern poetry and longs for an aesthetic commitment and for radicalness, supporting a return to the "more irrational elements of poetry" as an antidote for the generalized conformism of the present imitators of the *poesía de la experiencia*.

In his well-informed essay, Darío Villanueva describes the evolution of the Spanish literary system, which he construes as a set of functional relationships that engage writers from both sides of the Atlantic. His essay examines the cultural crossroads at which diverse literary practices intersect, and are judged in terms of their value to the whole. In other words, Villanueva develops and supports "a conception of literature which . . . includes multiple perspectives that crisscross and necessarily have implications for each individual life and for the history of different peoples." Villanueva states that we may legitimately speak of a coherent literature in Spanish that spans two continents, and transcends a simple geographic definition. He supports this notion by claiming that few literatures are determined by such complex relationships between tradition and renovation, writers and audiences, centers and peripheries, models and exceptions, creators and mediators, censorship and freedom, critics and readers. "The Evolution of the Spanish Literary System" ultatimately defends the provocative thesis of a global and dynamic literature in Spanish, liberated from a specific national center. Darío Villanueva coincides with Victor Fuentes in the need to integrate Spanish literatures from both sides of the Atlantic in the future development of the literary system, understood as a dynamic system of reciprocal influences, which is at the root of the challenging project of Neo-Hispanism.

Writer and journalist Rosa Montero in her keynote address "Spain: No Man's Land" offered a critical review of the accomplishments and failures of Spanish society in the last two decades and outlined the challenges of the 21st century. Montero highlighted the great strides achieved by the consolidation of a democratic culture: political, linguistic and cultural pluralism, the incorporation of women into all spheres of public life, and the participation in the construction of the European Community, but Montero also noted the negative aspects: the loss of historical memory, the desintegration of the traditional social fabric, a pervasive noueveau riche mentality, and an ethical vacuum, which has resulted in a high level of corruption at all levels of society. Montero concluded asserting that we are currently in a hiatus, an absolute vacuum, a "no man's land between what we were and what we will become", fearing that we presently have "the worst of both worlds". But having come so far in such a short time, Montero is optimistic that a crisis of this nature provides a good ocassion for collective self-reflection and that Spain as a nation will be able to face the challenges of the 21rst century as a fully grown democratic society.

Manuel Vázquez Montalbán, the well-known Catalan author and *avant la lettre* pioneer of cultural criticism in Spain, was prevented from participating in the conference due to ill health. His lucid reflections on the role on the intellectual in contemporary culture are excerpted from an interview with the author by José Colmeiro in the **Postscript** to this volume, "¿Qué pueden los intelectuales?", which offers complementary insights to Lourdes Ortiz's opening question "¿Qué puede la literatura?

The eclectic nature of this collection of essays reflects the interdisciplinary scope of the **"Spain Today"** symposium and shows the diverse critical practices made possible under the rubric of Neo-Hispanism. These essays, however, are only a part of a much broader collective enterprise: the continued renovation of Iberian Studies. Among the shared preoccupations of all the contributors to this volume is the need to study the literatures of Spain within the larger framework of cultural production, to open the canon and to recover marginalized or silenced voices from oblivion by articulating the interrelationship of national and transnational cultures and by theorizing concepts of history, ideology, gender, and the dinamics of power relations. The editors hope that the publication of these essays from the first conference on Iberian cultural studies in the United States, will inspire new readings of contemporary Spanish culture and will ignite further explorations into the realm of Neo-Hispanism.

## ¿Qué puede la literatura?

Lourdes Ortiz

Poquísimo. Puede poquísimo. Pero también casi todo. ¿Transforma el tiempo, el mundo, los hombres? ¿Influye en la realidad y la modifica? ¿Puede aliviar el sufrimiento de los pobres de la tierra, saciar su hambre, remediar su injusticia?

... Aquella literatura del compromiso y los sesenta, los ¿qué hacer? sartrianos, en que crecimos, de una generación que se había quedado muda y balbuciente, tras el cúmulo de horrores de una segunda guerra. Literatura de combate o parpadeo de la angustia. Y la sorpresa colectiva de la caída camusiana o el estertor de estercolero de un hombre en un cubo de basura que esperaba inútilmente a Godot. Y allí en la torre de la aldea, en el último instante, el hombre como proyecto existiendo en su gesto, descubriéndose en su acto supremo y definitivo, como un eco tardío de todas las resistencias y preludio o apuesta por distintos paraísos posibles, aquí en la tierra, que podrían estar al alcance de la mano. Literatura militante o desencajada de nuestros más inmediatos maestros. ¿Qué puede la literatura? Literatura de compromiso o literatura social, panfletaria y triste de aquellos precursores de los sesenta -en nuestro país, digo- que quiso cantar la mina o la central eléctrica, la vendimia agobiante o la pesadilla industrial. O aquel realismo crítico de un tiempo de silencio que abrió los ojos y la letra a un modo posible de hacer, para acabar encontrando unas señas de identidad perdidas tras la baraúnda de nuevas amistades o de tardes vividas con Teresa. Contar. El compromiso con el propio texto, de nuevo el arte por el arte, decían los modernos -hijos de telquelismos y estructuralismos- tan atentos a la vida autónoma del lenguaje, desplegándose y dejando resquicios para sucesivas y múltiples exploraciones arqueológicas: la presencia del hueco significativa, de la ausencia. Del sueño transformador a la modestia de la página que de pronto se hace grandiosa y retiene el mundo sin saberlo, negándose a dar cuenta. Una generación del desencanto, experimental y transgresora, que acaba en manierismos y parlotea, confundido el norte: epígonos del juego y del malabarismo verbal, que se aferran a un pretendido formalismo, que se mira el ombligo y que narra la pura inanidad y el miedo, ignorando inútilmente ese principio soberano de que forma y contenido son dos rostros, Jano bifronte, indiscernibles. Y el paso de los deconstructores, que sondean, trocean, hincan la pica para ahondar en los márgenes o en la curvatura inaprensible, más allá del significado latente o manifiesto. El texto como organismo autónomo, multiplicándose en el lector que se hace cómplice. ¿No lo fue siempre? Mi camarada, mi hermano.

¿Qué puede la literatura? Hijos de nuestro tiempo y construidos, modelados con el humus de palabras, de sentidos que nos han precedido y nos acompañan. Tan próximos y tan antiguos nuestros antepasados, tan indestructible y tenaz ese vínculo maravilloso que nos ata a ellos y nos sostiene: la escritura. Lo importante al final, como decía Marx -¡qué fuera de modas queda el citarle!- no es tanto cuales eran las condiciones sociales que permitieron que en un momento dado se alzara el Partenón, sino por que todavía hoy sigue conmoviéndonos. ¿Qué es eso que nos conmueve y que forma una línea invisible y resistente a través de las sucesivas generaciones, anulando el tiempo? Las palabras. El ojo chisporroteante de Polifemo, la voz alterada de Medea, dando muerte a sus hijos, la rebelión de Antígona, la mirada inclemente de Electra, el amor, modificándose, creación cultural, y sin embargo siempre el mismo: el ámbito del deseo y de la ausencia congelado en la letra. Construidos de la materia del sueño, descubriendo en el otro, aquel lejano, los ecos y las palabras que nos permiten formular lo que pensamos, creemos, añoramos: las lágrimas de Werther, la desolación impotente de Ana Karenina, la contundencia fría y cálida al tiempo de Quevedo, polvo enamorado, cenizas que tendrán sentido, el arrobo de Julieta, el arrebato lúcido de Melibea, allá en lo alto, la sensualidad gozosa de Anacreonte o de Omar Kayan, la impotencia circular de Kafka. Caudal de palabras que nos configuran y que, como un milagro, vuelven a abrirse y a proyectar sentidos en cada nueva lectura: temblamos con Madame Bovary, reconocemos a la dama negra, nos perdemos en el laberinto y en el túnel, tras sudar con esa extraña conspiración de ciegos, cruzamos los mares y sentimos la zozobra de Conrad, el desafío de Melville. Luchamos con la ballena blanca y revivimos las convulsiones de Mister Jeckill, al desdoblarnos también nosotros -el Bien y el Mal, acogotándonos en el abrazo; añoramos el cuello de la bella o el hálito putrefacto del vampiro, lanzamos gritos de rebeldía junto a los bandidos de Schiller, penetramos en el mundo de los miserables, en las alcantarillas y en las cloacas de la mano de Hugo, para recuperar la alegría cínica del mendigo en la Opera de los tres centavos, su risa demoledora; seguimos las tribulaciones del niño y nos paseamos por la sórdida Inglaterra industrial y desalmada, acompañamos a Dickens por los pasillos de prestamistas y rencorosos abogados, vibramos con el lacerante estallido de Henry Miller y el pulso se nos acelera, volvemos a la melancolía amorosa de Safo y pesarosos, pero deslumbrados descendemos con Dante a los infiernos...

¿Qué puede la literatura? Pasajeros de un viaje brevísimo, multiplicamos el tiempo y el espacio, crecemos con los libros, nos desplazamos hacia adelante y hacia atrás, sentimos el vértigo y el ritmo del verso, la cadencia de las palabras, sonreímos ante la metáfora perfecta e inesperada. Tan pequeños y gigantes de pronto, volando con Simbad en la alfombra mágica, levantando tejados y penetrando en las guardillas, curiosos impertinentes levantando el velo de lo cotidiano, compartiendo la hilaridad de Scapin, sus burlas y sus muecas, luchando contra molinos de viento y asistiendo después al desconsuelo de Sancho: "No se muera vuesa merced". Pasear por los salones, sorprender al alcahuete, al frívolo, al avaro, al melancólico, subir a los palacios y bajar a las cabañas, aturdidos por la galanura narcisista de Don Juan, presenciar la caída de las revoluciones y el fracaso de los anhelos, mientras sufrimos una educación sentimental, recorrer el campo de batalla con el entusiasmo juvenil de Fabrizzio del Dongo y compartir los ahogos y calores de la Sanseverina o la ternura sin finalidad de la Bovary. Descubrirnos a la puerta del castillo o en los pasillos laberínticos y llenos de polvo de un proceso sin fin, recorrer las callejuelas tortuosas de Alejandría en pos del cuerpo joven y canalla y suspirar junto a Cavafis por la llegada de los bárbaros liberadores. ¿Hay quien de más? La literatura lo puede todo y no puede nada. Es la materia del sueño, congelada en las letras. La bola mágica de todos los deseos; el pulso de los tiempos, donde quedan destiladas ideas, mundos, formas de vida y la variedad multiplicada de los comportamientos y los pueblos. Es por tanto también documento. Pero eso es lo de menos. Lo demás: es parte del alma colectiva, del espíritu absoluto, creciendo y transmitiéndose, fortaleciéndose y desmayándose, encarnándose de nuevo en cada uno de nosotros, tan iguales y tan distintos. "En esto veo, Melibea, la grandeza de Dios". El dios, hecho palabra, la palabra que nos hace como dioses, creando al mundo a nuestra imagen y semejanza. En el principio fue el verbo. Y gracias al verbo, la literatura.

No se si habré contestado la pregunta.

# I. Literature and History: New Critical Perspectives

# More than Three Forms of Distortion in 20th Century Spanish Literary Historiography: Counterpoint Alternatives

Víctor Fuentes
University of California, Santa Barbara.

To write a contemporary literary history attempting to reflect the complex and diverse framework of 20th century literature has proven to be an almost unattainable task, in any language or culture; the genre is in danger of being displaced by the encyclopedia. The attempts to write a literary history in our century have been, in one way or another, derivative ramifications of 19th century literary histories, constructed by the nationalist burgeoisies on the idealist presumptions of Modernity: the lineal progression of history, the unveiling of a suprapersonal idea or principle, be this the spirit or consciousness of a people, a nation or an era --classicism, baroque, romanticism-- and a teleology of a first origin and one finality.[1]

Although today these principles have collapsed, and to write literary history is almost a thing of the past, paradoxically we are witnessing a renewed interest in literary historiography. En 1991, David Perkins edited the volume Theoretical Issues in Literary History, followed by his own Is Literary History Possible? (1992). He answered affirmatively to this question, grounded in the postmodern sensibility to make the past present --but free of the dead weight of 19th century essentialism and nationalism propagated by modernity, free of that monumental reverence gravitating even today over so many 20th century literary histories. Perkins was convinced of the need to understand literary texts in the context of other texts and of the historical past.

In the field of Hispanism, the same renewed interest in literary history has been taking place. Inman Fox has recently written about the imperative of "a new literary history for Spain" (1991). In the same year of Is Literary History Possible?, a collection of essays on contemporary Spanish literary history was also published, with the works of critics such as Serge Salaum, Carlos Serrrano, Iris Zavala, and Mainer, among others. These essays problematized the limitations and distorsions of traditional historiographic concepts perpetuated by Spanish contemporay literary histories, such as periods, labels, and other canonical dogmas which have been hovering around since their origin in 19th century monotheist, centralist and nationalistic ideologies.[2]

My essay, in line with this revisionist trend, is a diachronic review of the major limitations and omissions of the now shaky canons of contemporary Spanish literary historiography. These canons are grounded in the outdated concept of "generation" and in formalist perspectives such as Ortega y Gasset's "dehumanization of art," and Juan Ramón Jiménez's "pure poetry." The somehow amazing longevity of such canons --from the 1920s until the present-- is due to the work of a critical axis formed by Menéndez Pidal, Pedro Salinas, Dámaso Alonso, Laín Entralgo, Guillermo Diaz-Plaja and a sequel of repetitive critics, supported by publishing institutions such as Espasa-Calpe, among others, which have succesfully linked the continuun of literary history to the ideology and values of the bourgeoisie (represented by the conservative liberalism of the 1930s, Franco's fascism and the conservative neoliberalism of the now ruling Spanish Socialist party).

In opposition to this official or canonical trend, this essay attempts to rescue other excluded or obscured options, remapping an alternative 20th century Spanish literary history, based on inclusion, but also in discontinuities, plurality, divisions, differences, and resistance. That is to say, a literary history in tune with the plural, divisional, and conflictive nature of the social and literary realities in Spain today.

Already in 1967, Keith Whinnon, in his Spanish Literary Historiography: Three Forms of Distortion, pointed out that the first of these distortions was due to the fact that "we write our histories of literature with an almost total disregard for history," which explains why we lack a "history of Spanish Literature based in historical criteria" (23).[3] Likewise, in 1992 Botrel called for a "historical history of Spanish literature": a history aimed at clarifing the conditions of production and reception of literary texts, in their dialectic relation with other texts and the changing and diverse social structures ("Pour une Histoire" 40, 36). This socio-historical textual approach proposed by Botrel, coupled with Robert Jauss's "horizon of expectations" and Bordieu's concept of "literary field" would yield great results if applied to contemporary history of Spanish literature. Inman Fox has expressed the need "to practice a 20th century Spanish literary history in Jauss's terms, attentive to the diachronic specifity of reception, and the social function of literary works and the process of canon formation" (17).

Contrary to these approaches, what has prevailed as the main a-historical instrument of 20th century Spanish literary historiography has been the exclusive and worn out tool of the "generation" concept, resting on its two canonical pillars: the generations of 98 and 27, and their sequels *ad absurdum* and *ad infinitum* (that of 36, 50, 68, 70, 80) which will soon turn upon itself when someone will invent for the end of our century a new generation of 98. In the last decades, several critics have written against the "generation" distortion -Ricardo Gullón (1969), John Butt (1970), Ramos Gascón (1989), Salaün (1992), Janet Pérez (1993), among others--[4], but none with the the forceful and categorical vehemence of Christopher Soufas:

> The generational model cannot be reformed; it must be abandoned. It is so deeply embedded in the critical consciousness that it will defeat all attempts at expanding the canon until we descredit it. It is elitist, chauvinistic, racist, and sexist, and ultimately grounded in the protofacism of the thirties from which it arose. (1991-92; 268)

Soufas is not mistaken, when he launches the charges of today's "political correctness" against the apparently innocuous generational model. We only could reproch him for having left out the most important of all charges, that of classist, which, in a way, subsumes all the others. Even a brief topological and geological survey of the perennial standing of the "generation" concept in the battlefield of 20th century Spanish literary history reveals that its proponents are --consciously or unconsciously-- guardians of the burgeoisie's order: an order as dubious in many moments of 20th century Spanish history as the literary canons favored. It is not difficult to establish with Foucault that the discourses of knowledge imposed by these critics are linked to the discourses of power, to the hegemonic domination of the burgeoisie.

Inman Fox has already documented how *Azorín*'s invention of the "generation of 98" took place in 1913, when he followed the doctrinary principles of Juan de la Cierva, a leader of the conservative party (12). De la Cierva's beliefs provided *Azorín* with the concept of the continuity of the Spanish spirit and tradition, where he was able to place the "generation of 98." Fox points out that "the generation of 98 as a fundamental and usable historiographic concept for a critical consideration of modern Spanish Literature dates back to 1934" (12). But what Fox does not reveal is that the "scientific" reworking of the "generation of 98" accomplished by Pedro Salinas in 1934 is imbued with a conservative ideology similar to *Azorín*'s.

1934 is the year of the October insurrection of Asturias, coupled with the nationalist uprise in Catalonia and followed by a bloody military repression lead by General Franco. At the same time that these historical events were taking place, Salinas, at the University of Madrid, was giving his seminar on "The concept of generation applied to that of 98," by means of which he sanitized from of all historical and social contagions the Spanish turn-of-the-century literature. Following the Germanic methodology of Julius Petersen and his generational method, Salinas enclosed that conflictive, diverse and complex period of Spanish literature under the guise of a unitary spirituality, branded with the seal of "casticismo" ("pure" and "chaste").[5] Salinas did not follow the conservative politician Juan de la Cierva, but the tradicionalist and ultraconservative literary critics Menéndez y Pelayo and Menéndez Pidal. He did not belong to a conservative party but, judging by his correspondence with Jorge Guillén, it is easy to infer that he had a true abhorrence of "the rebellion of the masses" on the rise in the socio-political and cultural arena of Spain in the late twenties and early thirties. He despised or ridiculed the writers who echoed that rebellion: Díaz Fernández and Antonio Espina, but also Rafael Alberti, García Lorca and Luis Cernuda. He wrote, "I fear that Federico [García Lorca] in his noble career of emmulating Rafael [Alberti] will fall in the same 'social' trap" (Correspondencia 171).

Salinas's essay on the "generation of 98," was probably destined to be a milestone of a proyected Spanish literary history, directed by Menéndez Pidal, of which Salinas would direct the modern and contemporary periods. Fortunately, one could say, that project did not materialize. Menéndez Pidal's and Salinas's monotheist essentialism could not render and account of the conflictive, diverse and pluralist expressions of life and literature of Spanish 20th century. Menéndez Pidal and Salinas, in spite of their solid reputation as literary scholars, ignored a necessary imperative that, already by 1910, Lukacs had laid for the literary historian; that of uniting two disciplines: aesthetics that deals with "the permanent," and sociology that concers itself with "the variable."[6]

Antonio Machado might have had in mind the failure of the Centro de Estudios Históricos, under the direction Menéndez Pidal and Salinas, in producing a literary history, when his Juan de Mairena, in 1936, ironically laments that "there is a need for a good handbook of Spanish literature . . . because we do not have anybody capable of writing it," and he adds:

> The truth is that we lack general ideas about our literature. If we had them, we also would have good handbooks and we could, also, do without them. I dont know if you follow me ... Probably not.

In the aftermath of the Spanish Civil War, Franco's censorship made practically imposible any attempt to write a contemporary literary history. For the Franco regime, in its first and darkest decade, history had ended with the crusades, an era which it tried to revive. After the long Fascist wave of barbarism --during which the majority of modern and contemporary writers were considered anathema--when the project of writing a literary history was restarted, the lack of ideas was abismally greater than when Antonio Machado had complained about it. When the time came to rejoin the "Free World," the official culture turned to the blueprints of the idealist proyects of Menéndez Pidal and Pedro Salinas and rebuilt the monumental ruins of their literary historiography. Their ahistorical conception of Spanish literature interwoven with the thread of a traditional, spiritual, centralist, and unifying continuity was well suited to General Franco's delirious ideological pastiche "por el imperio hacia Dios". Actually, this rescue operation underscored--rather than the continuity of our literary history--the continuity of the bourgeoisie in power throughout the century, with the tragic exception of the Spanish Civil War where, in the Loyalist zone, this continuity was interrupted. This was reflected in the rise of a national popular conception of literature.

In 1947, the publisher Espasa-Calpe initiated its multi-volume History of Spain, under the direction of Menéndez Pidal, who also wrote the prologue --probably the one that he had written in the 20s for his own failed literary history-- for the six volumes of Historia general de las literaturas hispánicas, under the direction of Guillermo Díaz Plaja, well thought of by the regime. Likewise in 1947, Laín Entralgo, then one of Franco's organic intellectuals, revived the concept of "the generation of 98", in a book by the same title where he astutely eludes any mention to the *Führer* long gone in Germany, adapting it to the Francoist totalitarian ideology and incorporating Salina's spiritualist rendering of those writers and his essencialization of Castille, as the backbone of the Spanish Nation. In 1951, Díaz Plaja published his Modernismo frente al 98, where he developed another ideologically flawed critical concept of Pedro Salinas, paradoxically conceived in America in 1940; his understanding of the problem of *Modernismo* "as the conflict between two spirits", "the materialist, sensual and care-free afirmation of life," on behalf of the Hispano-American writers and the "austere and serious spiritual problematic" of the Spanish writers of 98.

Maintaining this "continuist and exclusivist" historiographic tradition, Dámaso Alonso, after his visit to Salinas and Guillén in the United States, came up in 1949 with the other pillar of the ruinous monument of "generation": that of

27, which he constructed as a group of poet friends, with no political leanings, which dominated the field of Spanish Literature between 1920 and 1936. From then on, Spanish official culture has had very few ideas to offer in the realm of literary historiography, progressing from generation to generation, and repetition to repetition, guided by the demands of the publishing market. What is rather surprisinging (unless viewed from an ideological perspective) is that the mayority of the international hispanist establishement, with few exceptions, followed heed.[7]

The generational model defines this period in practically all literary histories and studies written in Spain and the United States. And what is even more astonishing in the democratic Spain of the 80s and 90s is that the same distortions remain standing. Looping the loop of the ideological continuum grounded in the second decade of this centuy, Espasa-Calpe published in 1993 the latest volume of History of Spain, a project begun under the direction of Menéndez Pidal in 1947, covering the period of "The Silver Age" of Spanish culture (another equivocal label) and the director of this volume was none other than Pedro Laín Entralgo.

To find traces of alternative options (to the continuum that incongrously merged the two equivocal labels of the all encompasing idealistic periodization of this century, "Silver Age" and "Post-Civil War Literature", which José Carlos Mainer extends up to the present time) we have to look for other repressed, silenced or marginalized genealogies. The same year, 1940, that Salinas published his Literatura española del siglo XX, (a preview of the contemporary history of literature he never wrote), the same publishing house of exiled Spaniards in Mexico, "Séneca," published España aparta de mi este cáliz (Spain take this cup from me) by César Vallejo. In Salinas' criticism of 19th century Spanish Literature, one can not find a single allusion to the socio-historical reality of Spain. By contrast, Vallejo's book of poetry is entrenched in the social reality and in the lives and sufferings of the people: it culminates the tendency of "social literature," that, in spite of its richness in the Spanish literary panorama of the 1920s and 1930s, has been practically erased from Spanish literary histories or marginalized as a minor and contaminated sub-genre.

Although España is a book of poetry rather than literary history, we find in it (better than in most of the above mentioned literary histories or ersatz manuals) a new remapping with alternatives to the distortions of 20th century Spanish literary history and the seeds for other writings or readings of that history.

In this Marxist text, firmly grounded in the Hispanic poetic tradition going back to Saint John of the Cross and, ultimately, the Bible, spirituality and consciousness are embodied in material terms. The national consciousness and spiritualities that in the critical works of Salinas or Laín Entralgo were abstract floating entities, in España, aparta de mí este cáliz appeared personified in concrete beings; men and women, aware of their class positions, figthing for their lives in defense of their repressed culture and subjugated discourses: people, for example, like Pedro Rojas, who used to write "Viban los compañeros," with a "b" and not with the orthographically correct "v," or guerrilla fighter Lina Odena "en pugna más de un punto con Teresa" (challenging Teresa of Avila in more than one point). Although in this text, Madrid and Toledo are mentioned, the center is in the periphery: in Guernica, Bilbao, Santander, Málaga, Gijón, Aragón, Extremadura. This fact implicitly undermines the myth of Castile as the central core where the vital and literary essence of Spain resides. In literary terms this points out to the fact that a literary history of Spain can not be complete without the literatures in Basque, Catalan, Galician, and without recognizing the specificities of other regional literatures.

While Salinas insisted in uniting all Spanish literature under Castilian hegemony, he also insisted in separating Spanish literature from that of SpanishAmerica. But, how can we segregate España, aparta de mi este cáliz from the main body of 20th century Spanish literature or even Vallejo's indigenist novel, Tunqsteno, written in Madrid by the great Peruvian writer? Both texts are intricately webbed in the social and literary texture of the Spanish society of that time. Likewise, the novel of Mariano Azuela, Los de abajo (The underdogs), when reprinted in Spain, in 1926, had a greater critical and public acclaim there than when first published in Mexico. It was the first novel written in Spanish of a series of very succesful anti-militarist novels advocating social revolution, such as Valle-Inclán's Tirano Banderas, Diaz Fernández's El blocao, and Sender's Imán.

All these works are part of that tendency in Spanish literature, beginning with Antonio Machado and Valle-Inclán in 1919 and 1920, followed by many professional writers and artists who directed their attention to the life and culture of the oppresed and repressed. That "march toward the people" produced a literary tendency antagonistic to that of "pure and formalistic poetry and literature," which, in Spain and in the 1920s and 1930s, was prevalent in the "horizon of expectations" of the Spanish reading public. A social tendency that has its masterpieces in poetry in España and in García Lorca's Poet in

New York, Picasso's Guernica in art, and that it counts with an important body of novels in which we have to include a pre-boom of Spanish-American novels, published in Spain, such as El águila y la serpiente y La sombra del caudillo, by Mexican author (nationalized Spanish) Martín Luis Guzmán, Las lanzas Coloradas, by Uslar Pietri, Don Goyo, by Agulera Malta and ¡Ecue-Yamba-Oh, by Carpentier.

This dominant literary trend, needless to say, was erased from memory by censhorship and the literary histories produced in Franco's Spain. José Manuel López Abiada has already written a detailed analysis of this phenomenon in his "De escritores silenciados y manuales de literatura." But what is more ominous --and a sad proof of the lasting effects of that eradication even after the demise of a particular political regime-- is the fact that contemporary critics in Post-Franco Spain have continued this distorsion. Such is the case of Luis de Llera Esteban (who had the praiseworthy intention of doing away with the concept of "generation" by replacing it with that of "tendency"), when he writes in 1993 that "el purismo" or purist literature was the dominant tendency in the 1920s and 1930s. He is not even aware of the antagonistic and, at the time, prevalent tendency of social literature, in spite of all the scholarly body of work already published.

España was published in Mexico by Republican Spaniards in exile, who, showing a greater tolerance than that existing in Franco's Spain, published in same year a book of liberal conservative ideology such as the one by Salinas and another one by a Marxist author such as Vallejo. There were many other exiled Spanish writers in other Latin America countries and in France. Taken as a whole, these exiles produced the most important body of Spanish literature and criticism of the period until the late fifties and early sixties when many of them began to publish in Spain. The main part of that moral and aesthetic continuity that Mainer sees in the Spanish literary trayectory between the thirties and the sixties, if it were to exist, would have to be found in that literature. It is time to reintegrate that complex, diverse and rich heritage of exile literature to the body of contemporary literary Spanish history.[8] Until now, it has been confined to a label and relegated to the remote ghetto of "literatura del exilio," at times even without the adjective "Spanish," and as such reduced to one or --at best-- a few short chapters in literary histories of Spain. Franquist censorship and their intellectuals, such as the literary historian Torrente Ballester, took vengeance on these writers (including conservative liberals, like Salinas) by erasing even the mention of their names.

This practice also left a mark that endures until today. In one of the most recent --if not the most-- literary histories, that of Oscar Barrero, Historia de la literatura española contemporánea 1939-1990, the "exiled writers" altogether take up two and a half pages, while Jardiel Poncela by himself occupies ten pages, in what appears to be a posthumous joke in line with Poncela's sense of humor.

Returning to our study of the ideological implication of literary historiography, it is quite revealing to recall that it was the researchers at the Centro de Estudios Históricos, dissidents from the traditionalist, "casticista" and "castellanizante" conception of the two Menéndezes, such as Américo Castro, Federico de Onís, José Montesinos and Vicente Llorens, who proposed new theories of literary history where aesthetics, history and sociology are intertwined. This group of liberal critics, but preoccupied with social issues (and that was the reason of their exile) produced historiographic concepts freeing our literature from the barren canonical dead end to which it had been condemned.

In 1923 Federico de Onís devoted himself to the study of "contemporary literature in Spanish language" (note that he is refering to a literature written in a particular language and not the literature of a particular nation, and therefore he studied Spanish and Spanish American authors side by side), guarding himself against the critics whom he called the "seudo tradicionalistas" when he wrote: "There will be those who, because of this, will classify us as radicals and anti-tradicionalistas" (361). In 1934 in his introduction to his Antología de poesía española, de Onís includes both men and women, Spanish and Spanish American poets, and he proposes a definition of "modernismo" (without distinguishing between 98 and "modernismo") as a period or spirit of the period known as Modernity, which spans from 1880 to the 1930s. He offers one of the first definitions of what today is considered the period of international modernism, a periodization widely accepted by European and North American critics. The work Modernism. A guide to European Literature 1890-1930, edited by Malcom Bradbury and James McFarlane in 1976, marks almost the same dates for international modernism as Federico de Onís's earlier study.

Américo Castro elaborated during his years of exile his theories of the hybrid cultural history of Spain, acknowledging the Christian, Jewish, and Arab realities of Spanish history, which make him a precursor of current cultural studies and multicultural theories.

All those possibilities of renovation and creation between the civil war and the subsequent exile were lost with their authors around the world and, in Spain, they were silenced and ridiculed until the present day. Nevertheless, any attempt to reconstruct a history of 20th century Spanish Literature would have to take into account the concept proposed by Federico de Onís's regarding the genealogical periodization "Modernismo"/ "Postmodernismo" and, following Américo Castro, would have to read a literary work in its broadest cultural context. Likewise, Juan de Mairena and España, aparta de mi este cáliz would be crucial points of reference for that possible literary history. The Peruvian's book, living in Paris but with his body and soul in the battlefields of Spain, first published by Republican soldiers in Catalonia, was already a part of the dead Republican soldier's body ("un libro, atras un libro, arriba un libro/retoño del cadáver muerto"). España, aparta de mi este cáliz, a collection of poems about life and death, belonging perhaps to Vallejo, to the militia soldier or to us, could well be the key to a contemporary literary history which has been denied, mutilated, never written, but waiting for its reader-writer.

## Notes

[1] See Julio Rodríguez Puértolas's essay "La literatura marginada" on the Catholic and "castellanizante" imprint given to Spanish literary historiography by its fathers Menéndez y Pelayo and Menéndez Pidal.

[2] There have been several collective works in the last decade which have underlined the need for a revision from new perspectives of Spanish literary historiography. I will mention some studies, in addition to the French text above mentioned: the issue of the Revista canadiense de estudios hispánicos (Spring 89); the group of hispanists from the University of Minnesota, The Crisis of Institutionalized Literature in Spain, edited by Wlad Godzich and Nicholas Spadaccini (1988) and the study edited by Bridget Aldacara, Edward Baker and John Beverly, Texto y sociedad: problemas de historia literaria.

[3] The other two "forms of distorsion" discussed by Whinnom could also be added: aesthetic (and ideological) biases of the present day critic when judging the works of the past, and the puritan reservation towards erotic or pornographic literature rejected as "obscene". When Franco's regime attempted to revive Phillip II

and the Counter-Reformation, official literary historiography and censorship revived this distorsion with a vengeance. We might want to recall the censored passages of Tiempo de silencio.

[4] Janet Pérez in regards to the generation of 27 asks: "But where are the women contemporaries of these poets?" (40), and she lists the names of neglected women poets Clementina Arderiu, Ernestina de Champourcín, María Teresa Roca de Togores, Cristina Arteaga, and Carmen Conde.

[5] Some aspects of the protofacism that Soufas associates with the generation concept could also be seen in Salinas's definition of the concept with his continuous allusions to the *führer*. It is an unfortunate invocation, to say the least, especially if we take into account that his Spanish counterpart, *el caudillo*, initiated in Asturias his general rehearsal of the Spanish Civil War at the same time as Salinas's book was written.

[6] Frontiseck W. Galán reflects Luckacs's thought in Las estructuras históricas (21).

[7] There are exceptions among the "unorthodox" critics since 1968. The most important of these is La Historia social de la literatura española by Carlos Blanco Aguinaga et al., which, in spite of the shortcomings or limitations of every social history of art or culture, truly hit the mark, and therefore, originated hostile responses. Likewise, in contemporary hispanic studies, there are other exceptions, such as British hispanist Barry Jordan, whose text Writing and Politics in Franco's Spain vindicates the critically despised "social novel" of the 1950s; or Soufas's text, where he studies the poets of 27 dividing them according to their ideologies. Soufas meticulously analyzes Salinas and Guillén's poetry coinciding with what I am proposing in this essay about the ideological underpinnings of their principles of literary criticism.

[8] Surprisingly a literary historian as sharp and sensitive to the social mediations of literature as José Carlos Mainer, in his text La corona hecha trizas (1930-1960) traces the historical development of Spanish literature from 1930 to 1960 to corroborate "its intense moral and aesthetic continuity," but excludes the Spanish literature of exile.

Works cited:

Aldaraca Bridget, Edward Baker y John Beverley, eds. Texto y sociedad: problemas de historia literaria. Amsterdam-Atlanta: Rodopi, 1990.

Barreo Pérez Oscar. Historia de la literatura española contemporánea (1939-1990). Madrid: Fundamentos, 1992.

Blanco Aguinaga, Carlos, Julio Rodríquez Puértolas, Iris Zavala. Historia social de la literatura española. Madrid: Castalia, 1981-83.

Bradbury, Malcolm and James McFarlane, eds. Modernism. A Guide to European Literature 1890-1930. London: Penguin Books, 1976.

De Onís, Federico. "El problema de lo contemporáneo." España en América. San Juan: Ediciones de la Universidad de Puerto Rico, 1953. 355-361.

Fox, Inman. "Hacia una nueva historia literaria para España," Dai Modernismi alle Avanguardie. Ed. M. Caterina Ruta. Palermo: Flaccovio Editore, 1991. 7-17.

Galán, Frantisek. W. Las estructuras históricas; el proyecto de la escuela de Praga 1928-1946. Mexico: Siglo XXI, 1988.

Godzin Wlad y Nicholas Spadaccini. Eds. The crisis of Institutionalized Literature in Spain. Minneapolis: The Prisma Institute, 1988.

Jordan, Barry. Writing and Politics in Franco's Spain. Londres and Nueva York: Routledge, 1990.

Llera Estebán, Luis de. "De las generaciones a las tendencias: una propuesta cultural neo-orteguiana." New History, Nouvelle Histoire, Hacia una nueva Historia. Ed. José Andrés Gallego. Madrid: Actas, 1993.

López de Abiada, José Manuel. "De escritores silenciados y manuales de literatura. En torno a los novelistas marginados de la generación del 27." Homenaje a Gustav Siebenman. Eds. José Manuel López de Abiada y Augusta López Bernasocchi. Madrid: José Esteban, editor. 1986.

Machado, Antonio. Juan de Mairena. Espasa-Calpe, Madrid, 1973.

Mainer, José-Carlos. La corona hecha trizas (1930-1960). Barcelona: PPU: 1989.

Pérez, Janet. "On Misapplication of the Generational Label." Letras peninsulares 6.1 (1993): 31-50.

Perkins, David. Is Literary History Possible?. Baltimore: The Johns Hopkins University Press, 1992.

Rodriguez Puértolas, Julio. "La literatura marginada, el papel de la crítica y otras cuestiones." Revista canadiense de estudios hispánicos 3 (1989): 429-46.

Salaüm Serge y Carlos Serrano. Ed. Histoire de la littérature espagnole contemporaine. XIXe-XXe siècle. Paris: Presse de la Sorbonne Nouvelle, 1992.

Salinas, Pedro y Jorge Guillén. Correspondencia (1923-1951). Barcelona: Tusquets, 1994.

- - -. Literatura española. Siglo XX. Mexico: Séneca, 1940.

Soufas Christopher C. "A Relaxed Response to the Review of Conflict of Light and Wind by Margaret Persin. Siglo XX/20th Century (1991-92): 267-269.

- - -. Conflict of Light and Wind. The Spanish Generation of 1927 and the Ideology of Poetic Form. Middletown: Wesleyan University Press, 1990.

Vallejo, César. España, aparta de mí este cáliz. Mexico: 1940.

Whinnom, Keith. Spanish Literary Historiography: Three forms of Distortions. Exeter, University of Exeter, 1967.

# Reading Fiction through Historiography (or Vice Versa?)

David K. Herzberger
University of Connecticut

Traditional studies of source and influence in literary scholarship have generally grown from two interrelated purposes: 1) to locate the point of origin of a particular piece of writing; and 2) to identify explicit transtextual references that prop up and shape a work's meaning(s) (what Michael Riffaterre refers to as the obligatory intertextuality of reading).[1] What a text "means" in a given context may of course be enriched by the plurality of texts associated with it, a process of interconnecting that is shaped by a reader's experience and desire for sense-making. This desire implies intentionality, a critical responding that allows readers to work through a text by laying it against other texts, which in turn produce and authorize certain codes of meaning. While in theory a text consists of the forms and meanings of a mosaic of previous texts unnamed and unnamable, in critical practice intertextual study assumes the form of specific impositions: new meanings are revealed, historical filiations discerned, and structural similarities laid bare across works that the reader chooses to summon forth (what might be termed the "reasoned aleatory" nature of intertextuality).

The propping of one discourse against another, and the forced coalescence that is implied, urges a realignment of the potential meanings of each. But there are two obstacles to overcome if we assert such a realignment. First, we must be able to articulate our perception of similitude in dissimilitude--much like in metaphor--that has compelled us to place texts together that might normally remain apart. Recent critical writing (primarily by New Historicists) on the dissolution of traditional distinctions between discourses has laid the groundwork for such a possibility. Second, there is no theoretical or practical requirement for the realignment of works to occur only through specific texts. Indeed, it is possible to identify a set of discursive practices related to one generic category and lay these against the discursive practices of another, and thus change the signifying codes of each. This allows a diversity of potential textual relations that encourages the intersection of texts previously denied congruity or even juxtaposition. It therefore creates what may be termed an intertextual defamiliarization. This idea is especially pertinent to the remarks that I wish to make on the relationship between historiography and fiction in a general sense and, more concretely, between historiography and fiction in Francoist Spain.

I have often heard colleagues remark (both literary specialists and non-specialists) that they have read a novel in which the past time of "real life" (what we commonly call history) has played a prominent role. This generally means that a fictional character or characters is located within the world of people and events that we know to have really existed--e.g., World War II, Napoleonic France, the Spanish Civil War. If the novel bears the marks of authenticity in its representations, if dates, places, and events seem to be right based upon our general knowledge, the inevitable question arises: did things really happen that way? If the reader is persistently curious, he or she will probably pursue the matter of "truth" outside of fiction, often by consulting a book in which the authority of truth is expected to be found--a book of history. We know that the ethical impetus and intention of historians ought to be rooted in a commitment to the truth--to pinning down facts, to getting things right based upon research done in the real world. We of course understand that facts are not always what they appear to be, that documents, statistics, and archives can be deceitful. But there exists an implied contract between historians and their readers that information gathered through research will be presented as faithfully as possible, hence all inferences made by readers will, in theory, be verifiable by historically determined events that occurred outside the text. In this sense history claims for itself the unique privilege of putting us into authentic contact with life through the medium of the objective historian and the objectifying authority of language.

In contrast, there is no such moral or ethical imperative at work in the writing of fiction. Authors may use or ignore facts as they choose. They may draw together occurrences from the historical world and those purely invented. They may distort, invent, delete, or augment through the authority bestowed upon them both by tradition and convention. As a result, both common sense and, often times, the need to act, to make a pragmatic decision based upon knowledge, generally lead us to rely upon historiography rather than fiction when we wish to use the past to take action in the present or when we wish to plan for the future.

Yet there is a crucial distinction to be made between, on the one hand, using the past in one way or another as a given content that can be inferred to be true as a representation of specific occurrences (e.g., Ferdinand and Isabel were really married, the Spanish fleet suffered major losses in 1588, the Spanish Civil War broke out in 1936) and, on the other, making what Henry Steele Commager has called a "usable past." The making of a past, with its implicit emphasis on constructing, compels us to question, first of all, for what purpose the past is made and, second, to scrutinize the building materials that will be used and how those materials create meaning and significance. In the case of the Franco regime, the purpose is quite clear: the State uses the past both to proclaim that it has fulfilled Spain's historical destiny in the present and to give moral legitimacy to its vision of the future. It is important to understand, however, that the Regime's appropriation of history for its own use is generally not carried out to dispute the so-called "facts" of the Spanish past or even, curiously enough, to dispute the long-held views of liberal historians that Spain had been mired in economic and social decay for centuries. Instead, historians of the State set out to establish a normative set of strategies that define a particular <u>concept</u> of historiography. The consequences of this intentionality are two-fold: 1) Francoist historians impose a universalist perspective on the Spanish past, hence their assertions are presented as if "naturally" embedded and available in life, unfettered by contingency and ambiguity; and 2) historians of the Regime evoke a mythic past as the coequal of truth, thus historiography not only imposes sameness, it also disallows difference.

The Regime's historiographic claims upon truth are buttressed by a reflection theory of narration that locates the critical representational structures of history in the world. That is to say, the story that historians tell about the past is the story that has to be told because it is already embedded in events as they unfold in time. But the insistence by Francoist historians that they reflect the given story of Spain is in fact only half the story. They demand privileged access to the real, as if it were "there" in the world, able to be fully represented. But curiously, they proceed in an overtly intertextual way. The iconic voice of myth that lies at the center of their historiography emerges less as a consequence of the appropriation of stories found in life than as a contrived component of intertextual connections. Their historiography is therefore ultimately sustained through relationships established with previous discursive practices and the meanings that have been associated with them. In a practical sense, this means that Francoist historians give prominence to the discursive elements of historiography (quite unintentionally, I am certain), so that the internal mechanisms of composition and the relationship among texts command equal recognition with the external occurrences of fact.

There are many instances of the intertextual foundation of Francoist historiography--Menéndez y Pelayo, for example, or the Russian exile Nicholai Berdyaev, resonate with deep authority in the mythmaking discourse of the Regime.[2] I do not wish to belabor the point with numerous references to this intertextuality, but simply want to point out that the strategies used by historians of the Regime are consistent: they co-opt the texts of others and make these texts precursors of their own historiography. Menéndez y Pelayo is particularly important to Francoist historians. For example, writing in 1949 in Arbor on the broad reach of Menéndez y Pelayo's ideas, Florentino Pérez Embid offers in brief the strategy for appropriating the Spanish thinker. He argues that Menéndez y Pelayo reveals the "concepción permanente de la existencia española," shows the "unidad superior" of the nation, and underscores Spain's "vitalidad histórica" (153). In other words, Francoist historians proclaimed the permanence of Menéndez y Pelayo as an intellectual icon and announced their attachment to his thinking. More importantly, however, they usurped from him what was unique and individual and converted him into a Francoist avant la lettre.[3] In this way Francoist historiography ascribes to the meaning of history the concept of a single truth rooted in a sacralized text and, in doing so, allies itself with permanence and stability. The historiography of the Regime therefore actually comes to constitute the past and acquires the standing of a powerful ideolect. The master narrative of Francoist historiography absorbs diversity into its discursive grid, which has the practical result of suppressing difference.

There is, however, a relentless perturbation to such thinking that compels openness. The critical pragmatics of intertextuality proposes that it is possible (and necessary) to perceive narratives in relation to other narratives. This idea, as we have seen, is used by historians of the State to make their discourse appear inevitable within Spanish orthodoxy and to create their own precursors. In the context of narrating the past, this pragmatics of intertextuality means that any narrative that sets out to recover or reinvent the past in Francoist Spain immediately stands in <u>some</u> relation to the constituent texts of the Regime. The Regime's texts in fact become the defining marker of all other such narratives precisely because of the intention to end discussion of the past. And while the Regime sought to diminish the vulnerability of its authority through the creation of its metadiscourse, it could not impede the flow of counterdiscourses without the total suppression of writing itself.

There are any number of such discourses that circulate in the 1950s through the 1970s (for example, the novel of social realism, the novel of memory, the memoir, the high modern novels of writers such as Juan Benet or Luis Goytisolo, and postmodern fiction). These discourses stand in relation to Francoist historiography in a diversity of ways because of the diversity of their own discursive practices. But it is the overriding desire in nearly all of this fiction to "think" historically that gives them special pertinence. And what is more, this thinking goes on discursively. These works do not contest Francoist historiography on the battleground of truth of occurrence, hoping to gain small bits of the historical terrain here or there. Instead, when laid over and against the discourse of Francoist historiography, these works directly assault its expressive center--the monological discourse that is concerned with announcing and embodying a single historical vision. When read against Francoist historiography these narrations emerge as places of dissension, rich with subversive impulses, sharp discontinuities, and temporal aporias.

I would like to discuss very briefly the strategies of this intertextuality, using examples from the postmodern fiction of Gonzalo Torrente Ballester (some of which was written near the end of Franco's rule and some after his death). Postmodern fictions are particularly troublesome when it comes to history, since on the face of it they generally deny the possibility of writing history with a narrative discourse whose referent can only be other discourses. It is precisely this insistence on the discursive core of history and fiction, however, that makes Spanish postmodern fiction such a powerful source of intertextual dissidence in relation to Francoist historiography. It discredits not only the concept of a master discourse capable of conveying the truth about the past, but also undermines in a specific way the myths of history created and sustained by the State.

The postmodern novels of Gonzalo Torrente Ballester--e.g., Fragmentos de apocalipsis (1977); La isla de los jacintos cortados (1980); La rosa de los vientos (1985)--purposefully embody intertextual connections between fiction and history.[4] These novels are about history in the sense that they scrutinize the narrative paradigms used to evoke the past, and they challenge any discourse that asserts itself as mimetically complete. For example, in Fragmentos de apocalipsis Torrente Ballester does not call forth Spanish history per se as the referent of his work--the novel attempts to tell the fantastic story of Villasanta and its inhabitants. But Torrente Ballester does raise general questions about the conceptual frame of narration as it relates to the underestanding of time. Most importantly, however, Torrente Ballester asserts in Fragmentos the idea of history as a question that generates other questions, which generate still others, thus creating a never-ending concatenation of incongruities that shake the safe zone of truth to its very core.

Torrente Ballester opposes the discursive narrowness of Francoist historians in several important ways. Rather than condense heterological voices into a hypostatic oneness (as does the Regime), his purpose is to sustain difference and nuance. In La rosa de los vientos, for example, he shows how the past always remains open to the oxymoronic imperative of what might be termed "disparate repetitions." As the narrator of the novel suggests, "me parece que la historia de mi destronamiento voy a tener que contarla varias veces, aunque confío en que de un modo distinto cada una de ellas; quiero decir, las mismas cosas con distintas palabras y desde puntos de vista variados" (26). Rather than condense the past into a single story, thus ridding history of complexity and difference, Torrente Ballester recognizes that the individual narrator is caught up in time (history) and thus subject to the contingency of storytelling and the diversity of its potential voices.

In his speeches on the Spanish past, Franco often declared that the history of his nation must necessarily be viewed as the accumulation of heroic deeds. In August of 1947, for example, he proclaimed that, "Todo lo grande que existe en España no ha sido obra de la casualidad: ha sido obra de hidalgos, de santos y de héroes, fruto de grandes empeños, de minorías selectas, de hombres elegidos. . . " (96). In sharp contrast, Torrente Ballester suggests in his writing that the "truth" of heroism is not naturally embedded in the world, a story waiting to be told by the perceptive historian. Instead, the very concept of a heroic past is a construct rooted in a temporally motivated desire and shaped by the words of a particular narration: "La historia la hacen los héroes, y los héroes son, a fin de cuentas, nada más que nombre y facha, que palabra y retrato" (Isla 255). Torrente Ballester's assertion of the preeminence of the word in the construction of history does not seek to show that heroism is a fraud, or that it should be excluded from our understanding of the past, but rather that it is a conceit shaped and defined by narration.

The disintegration of a unified voice (and therefore of the metanarrative conception of history) informs much of the recent fiction of Torrente Ballester, but is perhaps most acutely pertinent to the narration of Fragmentos de apocalipsis. The narrator's recurrent insistence that he is made only of words (e.g., he will create "un conjunto de palabras en el que estaré yo mismo, hecho palabra también" [132]) is a playful and parodic effort to show how referentiality cannot be tied to traditional concepts of representation and realism. For historiography, the emphasis on "words only" locates ambiguity at the root of narration and asserts that final truths are dispersed into the liquefying amorphousness inherent in all narrative endeavors. Hence Torrente Ballester does not set out to create a dialectic of self and other, with truth rooted in the former and deceit in the latter (as occurs in Francoist historiography). His purpose is to show the dynamism between self and other--how they intersect, separate, and divide into new selves and new others as the narrative frees itself from representation and asserts language as the informing construct of historical knowledge.

Francoist historians often created a mythic foundation for the past through the creation of binary oppositions. These oppositions generally represented Spanish history as a series of inclusions (e.g., Christianity, nobility, heroism) and exclusions (Judaism, Islam, secularism), which in effect guaranteed authenticity through consideration of the other. However, rather than create the dialectic with the purpose of arriving at a conciliatory synthesis, Francoist historiography negated the excluded component of the opposition in order to endow the past with sameness. In other words, one side of the dialectic was disallowed not from the very beginning, but only after it had been evoked and tainted with difference and inauthenticity.

In Torrente Ballester's Fragmentos de apocalipsis dialecticity is explicitly repudiated as a structure of organization. Early in the novel, the narrator (who is a novelist writing a novel) outlines a Manichean world defined by Good and Bad, Order and Chaos, framed within a heroic struggle. Such oppositions are an efficient way to make his point, he thinks, but he quickly realizes that the oppositions undermine the complexity that he seeks to convey. He therefore excludes them from his narrative. It is not the case, of course, that the narrator abrogates his authority to construct his work in one way or another. Rather, he understands that mimetic adequacy as a correlate of narration is only an illusion--it is always undercut by the shadowy zone that separates what is real from what is represented by symbolic discourse. In other words, the narrator understands that it is not life that has determined the dialectic of his novel, but rather the particular piece of literature that he has constructed. Hence the narrator disallows the opposition using the same inventive authority with which he created it. More importantly, however, the proposed oppositions offer a parallel discourse to Francoist historiography in their failure to achieve synthesis. But synthesis remains unachieved here for reasons of inclusion rather than exclusion. The text sustains difference and contradiction instead of suppressing them, thus the aleatory tensions and randomnes of narration do not fall victim to a single way of storytelling. Rather than advance meaning with a double face (one of which is stripped away as inauthentic, as in Francoist historiography), the novel proposes multiple faces which resist the totalitarian imposition of sameness in order to operate within the reversals and oscillations of difference.

I do not wish to suggest that fictional discourse in general, or the novels of Torrente Ballester in particular, stand free of relations of power and of powerful traditions of their own. Fictive discourse does not, and cannot, exist as an idealized, unfettered mediation of a universal, oppositional social voice. Torrente Ballester's postmodern fiction, as I have suggested, is in fact fully aware of how it constructs, transforms, and collapses its own center, only to begin again a process that necessarily repeats itself in order to enhance difference. And that is precisely the point. To read the past in historiography in general, to read the past in Francoist historiography in particular, and to read the past in fiction, is not just to read things described, but also to read systems of description. These systems remain intact intrinsically and acquire authority when each is left to stand by itself. But when these systems are read in relation to prior discourses or in relation to later ones, they change both in significance and meaning. I believe that if we are to comprehend the field of discourses in which the past is written in Francoist Spain, we must engage historiography through fiction--and vice-versa. For only then will we account for how texts relate to one another, and how they relate to (and shape) our understanding of the past.

## Notes

[1] See, for example, Riffaterre's "Production du texte: l'intertexte du Lys dans la vallée."

[2] Berdyaev was read mainly in French, Spanish, and Portuguese during the late 1930's and 1940's. His two most important works translated into Spanish during this period are La destinación del hombre (1948) and El sentido de la historia (1943). In 1938 he published in Spain Una nueva edad media and El cristiano y la lucha de clases.

[3] Francoist historians sanctify Menéndez y Pelayo and his writings in a number of ways, both in their own historiographic work and in essays that praise his insight into the Spanish past. See, for example, the special issue of Arbor devoted to Menéndez y Pelayo in 1956 (Vol. 34), in which the Spanish thinker is enthroned (ironically) as the paragon of scientific historians.

[4] These texts are published after the death of Franco in 1975, but their intertextual referent (perhaps "obligatory" in Riffaterre's sense) remains the traditions of historiography developed under Francoism. Torrente Ballester's ideas on history were developed fully during the years of the Franco regime, and he frequently posited historiographic norms that controverted those espoused by the State.

## Works cited

Commager, Henry Steele. The Search For a Usable Past and Other Essays. New York: Knopf, 1967.

Franco, Francisco. Franco ha dicho. Madrid: Voz, 1949.

Pérez Embid, Florentino. "Ante la nueva actualidad del `Problema de España.'" Arbor 14. 45-46 (1949): 149-59.

Riffaterre, Michel. "Production du texte: l'intertexte du Lys dans la vallée." Texte 2 (1984): 23-33.

Torrente Ballester, Gonzalo. Fragmentos de apocalipsis. Barcelona: Destino, 1977.

- - - . La isla de los jacintos cortados. Barcelona: Destino, 1980.

- - - . La rosa de los vientos. Barcelona: Destino, 1985.

# II. Spain on Screen

# Towards a New Transcultural Dialogue in Spanish Film

Jaume Martí-Olivella
Allegheny College

## I. The Ideological Debate: The Politics of National Identity.

I want to start this presentation by recalling the two most problematic and urgent cultural and political debates in Spain today: the need to rethink the concepts of nationalism and of feminism. Both concepts are often referred to in their most reductive and negative aspects. In saying "nationalism," we basically think of the most reactionary historical versions, either the conservative bourgeois model of the Nation-State or the fascist versions of National syndicalisms. As for "feminism," the word is almost always found in the context of a negative remark that alludes to a historically fixated moment: the radical movement of the sixties and seventies. I would like to suggest that in order to establish more solid political and cultural grounds on which we can all try and build a truly multicultural, heteroglossic and plurinational space, a space that we may still call Spain, we must come to a better understanding of these two terms. What is at stake, in my view, is our capacity to gain access to a truly "democratic culture."

I will , therefore, proceed by (re)presenting the debate around nationalism as it may be synthesized by two recent books published this year (1994) by Espasa Calpe in its "España Hoy" (Spain Today) series. I am referring to César Alonso de los Ríos 's Si España cae...Asalto nacionalista al Estado (If Spain falls... Nationalist Takeover of the State) and to Xavier Rubert de Ventós' Nacionalismos. El laberinto de la identidad (Nationalisms. The Identity Labyrinth). It is precisely Xavier Rubert de Ventós who describes what he understands to be a true "democratic culture." Let me quote him:

> Hasn't it been said that political democracy requires as its foundation a "democratic culture," a series of implied conventions on which it is based? Well then, this "democratic culture" is nothing else but the reconstruction at a "political" level of the traditional or metropolitan coherence

> on which the freedom of the smallest and/or homogeneous communities is based. A "democratic culture" with which the State has to compensate and supplement -- not to substitute -- that coherence in order to turn those small islands of autonomous identity into a continent of democratic freedom. (143-144)[1]

Rubert de Ventós' "continent of democratic freedom," in the Spanish context, implies the political recognition and "reconstruction" of those autonomous identities that have a "coherence" of their own. It is, simply put, the necessary recognition and reevaluation of a multicultural and a plurinational State, that may, ultimately, do away with the strictures and limitations superimposed by a Spain conceived as a traditional Nation-State. At the other end of this debate, I want to recall César Alonso de los Ríos' position. A position that he presents as a new "regeneracionismo" in front of the current decay of the very idea of Spain as a Nation-State. Let's hear his outcry:

> These kind of public officials who stubbornly reject reservations and problems (...) who have tried to substitute the word Spain with the euphemism of Spanish State. (...) How is Spain to fall if, in fact, for them it is already obsolete? Can these people say that the title of this book [If Spain Falls] is exaggerated and sensationalist who consider it rhetorical and abusive to use the term Spain as a Nation? Because if we cannot use the term Spain in its full sense, that is, as a Nation and as a State "tout court," that means we are not facing the possibility but witnessing a fact; it means that Spain has already fallen as an idea, a concept, a conscience. (12)

Interestingly enough, both Rubert de Ventós' and Alonso de los Ríos' narratives meet in their common gesture of blaming the State and its effort to strengthen itself by means of depriving its citizens of a collective memory. Thus, Alonso de los Ríos writes: "When Renan was writing that the nation is grounded on an amnesia, he was obviously referring to the origins. In Spain, however, this oblivion has acted on the present and has displaced and hurt a legacy that was most probably based on that amnesia. That is how the Nation and the idea of Nation has been hurt (19). Rubert de Ventós will elaborate precisely on Renan's "oubli," on that oblivion or amnesia that is culturally constructed. He writes that:

> The classical "contract of oblivion" becomes now the "oblivion of the original contract." What was before a gradual and dynamic process appears like a binary reality now: a civil and progressive Nation born from the Social Contract opposed to paroquial, atavistic and retrograde nationalisms. (...) This metamorphosis through which one moves from the sublimation of memory to its substitution is made obvious in the teaching of Language and History in the modern State: in its manufacture of a "universal language." (...) This is, ultimately, the culturicidal role of the school in the national State as Rousseau had already defined it in his Emile. (146-147)

Both authors coincide also in their opposite invocation of Renan's definition of a nation as a form of "daily plebiscite." For Alonso dc los Ríos: "Spain, despite the nationalists, is a nation that corresponds to the characteristics outlined by Renan: Spain has truly been the expression of "a vast solidarity," "a consensus" and the "desire, clearly expressed, to continue a life in common. (...) Spain, finally, exists as a Nation because it constitutes itself as a "daily plebiscite" (17). To this , Rubert de Ventós will say:

> "It's the people's "will" and not "the natural facts" -- one has argued -- that constitutes the basis of a nationalism understood like a "daily plebiscite." This is, indeed, the only way in which a liberal person may understand nationalism. And yet, this "will" is also a "fact" -- and a stubborn fact that cannot be erased by decree as one cannot sweep with a mop the waves of the sea. "E pur si muove" (142).

I cannot or perhaps do not want to close that dialogue, if indeed one can consider it a true dialogue; what I would like to do is to expand a bit the theoretical paradigm in order to include another voice, that of Benedict Anderson who, like Rubert de Ventós and Alonso de los Ríos, will work on the premise of Renan's definition to present his own, by now, famous formula, that of the nation as an "imagined community." Let me recall his words:

> In an anthropological spirit, then, I propose the following definition of the nation: it is an imagined political community. . . . It is "imagined" because the members of even the smallest nation will never know most of their fellow-members, meet them or even hear them, yet in the minds of each lives the image of their communion. Renan referred to this imagining in his suavely back-handed way when he wrote that 'Or l'essence d'une nation est que tous les individus aient beaucoup de choses in commun, et aussi que tous aient oublié bien des choses.' [Thus, the essence of a nation is that every individual has many things in common and at the same time that they have forgotten many things] (15)

If we are to follow Anderson's idea, and I am quite persuaded by his formulation, it seems necessary to conclude that the figure of the "daily plebiscite," if it exists, it does so only in the imagination and the mind of the people. It is something "imagined," or, in other words, something culturally constructed. Hence the enormous importance of cinema as a "dream-language." It is only in the context of those "imagined" discourses that individual voices and desires may be culturally inscribed against the monoglossic and "culturicidal" gestures of the hegemonic "national" powers.

In the case of Spain under Franco, cinema clearly played a crucial role as an alternative narrative in front of the dictator's monological "amnesia". Let us, for instance, remember Carlos Saura's excellent use of the amnesia motif in his allegorical <u>El jardín de las delicias</u> (Garden of Delights), as Marvin D'Lugo reminded us in his excellent book length study of Saura[2]. It is my contention that cinema has today even a greater historical responsibility, that of (re)creating a transcultural dialogue that becomes, in fact, a (re)construction of both our individual and our national identities. The two films I will be discussing in this essay: Pilar Miró's El pájaro de la felicidad (The Bird of Happiness) and Arantxa Lazcano's Urte Ilunak (The Dark Years), try to reconstruct precisely a personal past that has a collective and national significance.

## II. Towards a Transcultural Dialogue: Arantxa Lazcano's Urte Ilunak and Pilar Miró's El pájaro de la felicidad.

What have these two apparently disparate films in common? Why do I bring them together in this essay? First and foremost, because they constitute examples of gendered film discourses which establish the visual foundations for a new dialogue across Spain's different languages and cultures. Second, because I think they are among the most interesting illustrations of a cinematic return to music and poetry in the creation of personal narratives that are intertextually structured and that have a Jamesonian significance inasmuch as they make visible a national configuration through a private story.[3] In short, these two films are extremely personal and yet politically relevant and challenging, especially in the Spanish cinematic context, still dominated by impersonal sexual comedies and/or postmodern melodramatic "pastiches."

Both films, I would argue, respond quite interestingly to the new dynamics of micro and macro-regionalism as delineated by Marsha Kinder in an essay first published in the proceedings of the CINE-LIT conference and later incorporated in her volume Blood Cinema. The Reconstruction of National Identity in Spain.[4] It may be appropriate to recall her words here:

> While the United States has successfully marketed and naturalized its own national product as a global mass culture capable of colonizing the world, the Japanese have perfected the opposite strategy--the ultimate postmodernist simulacrum that imitates, improves, and thereby conquers and replaces the alien Other. Yet both models eradicate difference. In contrast, the European Community is developing a strategy that retains and highlights cultural diversity, and

> that is why the combination of micro- and macroregionalism is so central to its enterprise. (400)

In order to achieve or retain a personal idiom, in front of the hegemonic language of Hollywood, European cinemas try to reemphasize their particularities. Among these particularities, I want to underline the return to music and poetry, as if returning to a kind of cinematic origins, in order to create very intimate, almost confessional narratives, which, nevertheless, seem capable of reimagining the national communities that they allegorically represent. Among the most interesting recent examples that come to mind are the German film The Nasty Girl, directed by Michael Verhoeven, the Italian films Ciao Professore (Bye-bye Professor) by Lina Wertmüller and Stanno tutti bene (Everybody is fine) by Giuseppe Tornatore, the director of Cinema Paradiso, and the French-Polish Krzysztof Kieslowski's Three Colors trilogy, which has received great critical acclaim here in the United States. It is no coincidence, therefore, that Pilar Miró would hire the Catalan composer Jordi Savall to compile the excellent musical score of El pájaro de la felicidad. Two years before, Savall himself had been responsible for the musical soundtrack of Alain Corneau's intensely lyrical Tous les matins du monde (1991) ( All the mornings of the world). The leading poetic motif of that film: "tous les matins du monde sont sans retour," (all the mornings of the world never come back) is a clear influence on Miró's own nostalgic retrospection. Other than Alain Courneau's, Pilar Miró includes several poetic and musical intertexts in her film. Besides the obvious reference to Pío Baroja's elusive "pájaro de la felicidad," I find particularly significant the use of Dido's dramatic and beautiful final aria from Henry Purcell's opera Dido and Aeneas. The last sequences of the film, thus, manage to reverse the traditionally patriarchal "Liebestod" motif into Miró's affirmative version of the sacrifice of love. Indeed, Carmen's reclaiming of her own body, her newly accepted maternal role and her new life beyond her "social death" are all brilliantly counterpointed through Purcell's operatic intertext. Carmen's rich and difficult solitude, moreover, ressonates throughout the film by means of Angel González's lyrical intertext: "La soledad es como un faro certeramente apedreado, en ella me apoyo..." (Loneliness is like a lighthouse deftly stonewalled on which I lean). These lines amount to a visual and textual inscription of Carmen's (and Miró's) personal split between the need for silence and introspection and the commitment to public action, a contradiction that informs the central narrative of Pilar Miró's most lyrical film to date.

Having now established the context of this new European idiom, let me return briefly to Marsha Kinder's argument. She writes:

> Most important, because micro- and macroregionalism function co-dependently, fluidly shifting meaning according to context, they thereby serve as an effective means both of asserting the subversive force of any marginal position and of destabilizing (or at least redefining) the hegemonic power of any center. Once regional structures and the "center" come to be seen as sliding signifiers, then there is movement toward the proliferation and empowerment of new structural units both at the micro and macro levels. (389)

I would argue, concerning the two films considered here, that Arantxa Lazcano and Pilar Miró may be doing the same thing within the Spanish context. By articulating a local story into a national context and by bringing a "regional" language into a national circuit, they are both "sliding the signifiers" of center and margin, Interestingly enough, one of the few reviews published in Madrid of Urte Ilunak was entitled "Una historia local" (A local story). Esteban Hernández, its author, writes: "Shot in direct sound in Castilian and Basque in the area of Guipuzcoa, it is a local production that now enters a national market" (E3). The reviewer, therefore, wants to marginalize the film by alluding to its "local" origin while reinforcing the notion of "national" as only belonging to films shot in Castilian Spanish. The identification of language and nationality and the question of the hegemonic view can be best exemplified by the opposite reactions between a Basque viewer and two expatriate Spanish women who saw Urte Ilunak in the International Film Festival of Montreal. This was reported by Fernando Bejarano for "Diario 16:"

> The film is spoken mostly in Basque. This fact originated interesting opposite reactions in the

> viewings here in Montreal. On the one hand, a Basque viewer got very moved while listening to his language and gave a Basque flag to the director. On the other, two ladies, of a conservative outlook, complained bitterly. Those irritated ladies belong to the Spanish colony of Montreal and they said they came to see Spanish cinema. They found, instead, that part of The Bilingual Lover is spoken in Catalan. The Dark Years, however, was too much for them to handle. (39)

This reaction echoes a previous and more systematic one; the one received by Eloy de la Iglesia, another Basque director who brought the "marginal" and the "regional" into the "national" mainstream. In his groundbreaking study, Laws of Desire. Questions of Homosexuality in Spanish Writing and Film. 1960-1990, Paul Julian Smith describes it perfectly:

> In spite of his espousal of the newspaper form, de la Iglesia's treatment at the hands of the press during this period was brutal. . . . Some of the abuse is also motivated by anti-Basque racism: one squib mocks de la Iglesia for a project (later to metamorphose into El Pico) featuring a gay love story set in the Basque country complete with dialogue in euskera. The anonymous journalist states that other countries seek to conquer the international market, implying that Spanish directors waste their time on such minority projects. This was a curious complaint to make against the most commercially successful director of his time: homosexuality and regional identity would thus always seem to be marginal even when placed at the center of a mass culture. (130-131)

I want to argue that Arantxa Lazcano's and Pilar Mirós films not only follow up on that tradition. They, in fact, clearly problematize the common notion of a Spanish film by incorporating "marginal" languages in "non-marginal" contexts. I think they constitute precisely a new alternative in the process of recognition of our multicultural reality. In fact, as I have already suggested, they manage to articulate an extremely personal story into a large social structure, and the collective significance of their tales is achieved without having to have recourse to obvious allegorical constructions such as was the case, for instance, in Fassbinder's otherwise paradigmatic The Marriage of Maria Braun.

Arantxa Lazcano's Urte Ilunak introduces a (re)vision of the Basque cultural reality by presenting the story if Itziar, a girl growing up in the household of Juan Laza and Gloria Artegui, a family tormented by a sense of defeat and betrayal. Itziar's development is portrayed in powerful poetic images that illustrate her difficult and yet stubborn negotiation of a society that is oppressive in its linguistic polarization. Itziar's central question "zergati?" (Why?)--becomes Arantxa Lazcano's own interrogation of the strictures of a historical past that still looms large on the dramatic side of the struggle for cultural and political identity in the Basque country today. Pilar Miró's Carmen, the female protagonist of El pájaro de la felicidad, on the other hand, is an uprooted Catalan woman who has become a prestigious art restorer. She lives and works in Madrid. She is divorced and has an estranged son and a faltering relationship with a Catalan architect when we first encounter her on the screen. Soon, she will be raped, an external aggression that she will try to overcome by means of a complete withdrawal into herself and her own troubled past. Ultimately, Carmen's confrontation with her Catalan origins and her submerged homoeroticism will allow her to reach a deeper understanding not only of herself but of her historical context. An apparently trivial, and yet remarkable common point between these two films produced in 1993 is that they use subtitles in their original versions, thus presenting the transition between Basque and Spanish or Catalan and Spanish as if it represented a normalized plurilingual reality when, in fact, as I have argued, they are themselves an attempt to normalize that reality.

My last remark brings me full circle to the beginning of this presentation: what is the reality that these two films try to "normalize"? It is the reality of a shared political space, Spain, that still resists itself to be reimagined and thus represented as a plurinational, multicultural and heteroglossic community. The bilingual realities of both films become a strong political statement in our current historical moment, still characterized by the bitter debates surrounding the acceptance of such a multicultural reality. They underline a common goal to reimagine the different languages and cultures of Spain as an essential richness and not as a constant source of national struggle. Pilar Miró, whom nobody thinks of as having Catalanist inclinations, has been very clear in this respect. When talking about the incorporation of Catalan in her film, she said that: "In Catalonia I have wanted to find a landscape, a language and an atmosphere that I consider very beautiful. Often from Madrid, Catalan culture is perceived as something very remote and I think that is not the case" (Llopart 33).

Both Pilar Miró and Arantxa Lazcano flatly object to consider their films as representatives of a feminine/feminist cinematic discourse.[5] I think that their resistance betrays on the one hand a misconception of the very term feminism and, on the other hand, a defensive mechanism to oppose any essentialist reduction that might render them even more vulnerable in a male dominated milieu. As for the misconception, I see it as an example of their fixation on an outdated historical position concerning feminism. That this is a rather common position held even by progressive and intellectual women in Spain may be corroborated by the following words, written by Martha A. Ackelsberg in her Free Women of Spain:

> But I was most fascinated, intrigued, and perplexed by her attitudes toward feminists and feminism -- attitudes which were, in many ways, the mirror image of those which the young ones had of Mujeres Libres: "We are not -- and we were not then -- feminists," she insisted. "We were not fighting against men. We did not want to substitute a feminist hierarchy for a masculine one." (...) I was surprised by her assumption that "feminism" meant opposition to men or the desire to replace male hierarchy with female hierarchy. A product of the early feminist movement in the United States, I had always assumed that feminism meant opposition to hierarchies of any sort. (2)

Elsewhere I have argued that one of the most interesting and challenging developments in Spanish fiction written by women is their specular transgression of the traditional mirror repetition imposed by general patriarchal models and specially reinforced by Francoist ideology.[6] It is my contention here that such a gesture has finally arrived to the Spanish screen. Regardless of the degree of (un)self-consciousness, both Pilar Miró and Arantxa Lazcano create their own mirror images and indulge in a transgressive -- and indeed a feminist -- gesture, that of representing the personal as political, of constructing a national allegory by means of inscribing their most private emotions. In the case of Arantxa Lazcano's film, this collective significance was readily perceived in the Basque country, while it was ignored or criticized elsewhere. Thus, Francisco Marinero, in a review significantly entitled "Demasiada poesía" (Too much poetry) and published in the Madrid daily El Mundo writes: "The first and most obvious excessive thing of the film is to resemble a historical chronicle" (E2). Whereas Felipe Rius who writes in Basque for Egin says: "Arantxa Lazcano in her first film not only frames the events that happened to a girl, but some facts of the history of an entire people" (57).

Despite their directors' critical positioning concerning the possibility of a gendered cinematic discourse, I consider that both films constitute the clearest instance to date of such discourse in Spain. Thus, in assessing one of Pilar Miró's most productive contradictions, Juan Antonio Pérez Millán has written the following:

> Pilar Miró's cinema could not be understood were it not intimately connected to her global attitude towards life. An attitude that is determined, among other factors, by her visceral rebelliousness in front of anything imposed on her; by a peculiar need for self-assertion that pushes her to frontally oppose anything that is felt as an arbitrary imposition. That characteristic reaction . . . solidified . . . in a position that was then termed "engaged" and that in herself became compatible with a radical and rather contradictory individualism. As it is also contradictory her capacity to combine her tendency to rationalize everything, to present her arguments in a cold, even ruthless way, with her admiration for genuine tenderness and her recourse to emotion and feeling as the privileged form of

> communication. . . . Six long feature films have emerged from that constant struggle between ideas presented with a stubborness that borders on obstinacy and emotions that tend to surface as if they had been repressed, as if belonging to an old seated dream. (278-279)

It will be in Pilar Miró's seventh film, El pájaro de la felicidad, that Pérez Millán's accurate words will be especially significant. It is not until this film that Pilar Miró will confront directly those old seated emotions in her own self. Never before had the Spanish director been able to embody her critique of the surrounding violence in a format that allowed so clearly the inscription of her (homoerotic) desire. In fact, Pilar Miró's filmography has been largely characterized by two rather distinct cinematic discourses. On the one hand, there are those films that confront political violence directly, such as the controversial El crimen de Cuenca (The Crime of Cuenca) (1979), a film that bluntly represents political torture and indicts the "Guardia Civil," Franco's paramilitary police force; and Beltenebros (1991), Miró's forceful rendering of Antonio Muñoz Molina's homonymous narrative of political intrigues and betrayals in the context of the expatriate anti-Franco struggle. And, on the other hand, there are the films that inscribe the political through the personal. Among these, Gary Cooper que estás en los cielos (Gary Cooper who art in Heaven) (1980), Werther (1996) and El pájaro de la felicidad (1993), all are films that share a confessional tone, a poetic visual style and the specular gesture of inscribing Pilar Miró's own private story in social contexts of a general and collective significance. More importantly, for my argument here, they all have the same leading actress: Mercedes Sampietro who has been referred to by some critics as Pilar Miró's "fetish" actress. Mercedes Sampietro will, indeed, be Andrea Soriano, the television producer in Gary Cooper que estás en los cielos, and also Carlota, the pediatric neurosurgeon who will fall in love with her almost autistic son's tutor in Werther, and Carmen, the art restorer of El pájaro de la felicidad. This remarkable recurrence constitutes, in my view, Pilar Mirós self-conscious attempt to recreate her own image -- Sampietro does in fact bear a resemblance to the director. And in so doing, Pilar Miró is transgressing the specular limitations of a patriarchal (heterosexual) desire.

Miró's inscription of the personal as political is already obvious in Gary Cooper que estás en los cielos, where the director's own open heart surgery is represented in Andrea Soriano's discovery of an illness that forces her to confront the fact of her radical isolation in terms of the sudden decay of her own body. Similarly, El pájaro de la felicidad presents a strong and independent woman suddenly brutalized by an external, collective aggression. Carmen's rape, in fact, becomes the emblem to inscribe the decay of the body politique. Technically, Pilar Miró employs several significant "dissolves" in order to visually establish the notion of the progressive dissolution of a national discourse that had constituted her own.[7] It is the discourse of the Socialist party that is directly referred to and vexed by the Francoist mother during Carmen's return to her parent's home in Catalonia. Before that emblematic return, however, Miró shows us Carmen's desolate (self) questioning. In that "qué pasa?" addressed to the camera more than to Fernando, Carmen's lover, and that recalls Itziar's "zergati" (why?) in Lazcano's Urte Ilunak, Miró is condensing a personal and a collective crisis. The "dissolve" of Miró's public narrative echoes the dissolution/disillusionment of the alternative official narrative brought about by the Socialists' own decay. Carmen's sexual abuse is, therefore, a visible figuration of Pilar Miró's political victimization.[8]

At the end, however, what prevails is the new vision, or the revision, of her most tender emotions. As Pérez Millán has it: "In fact, Carmen's discovery of a new dimension in her interpersonal relationships, at the end of the script of El pájaro de la felicidad, points toward the development of a different alternative (275). This alternative is an exploration of the way out of a world presided over by a series of variations of the Hegelian master-slave dialectics. In Carmen's embrace of Nani, her daughter-in-law, Pilar Miró seems to embrace a different desire, a different tenderness, a newly recovered sense of human contact and pathos. As I have argued in another essay[9], Pilar Miró's quasi-ekphrastic use of Murillo's rendition of the Virgin Mary and of Saint Elizabeth amounts to a reversed "pietà". Thus, when Mercedes Sampietro tells Aitana Sánchez-Gijón that Murillo "wanted to portray the positive side of life", Miró is telling us and herself that the only way out is to try and find the non-confrontational other in others and in ourselves. It is the same gesture that unites Itziar and her newly found

Extremaduran friend Sofía as "blood sisters" in Urte Ilunak. Their sisterhood is a bond freely chosen and becomes a direct rejection of those other sisters, the nuns who imposed a linguistic union by violent coercion. Itziar's and Sofía's embrace constitutes, moreover, the culminating moment in Arantxa Lazcano's rejection of a violent society that scapegoats its children. In their moment of bonding, the two girls are initiated not only to the secret hidden by the allegorical tree -- a clear allusion to the Basque national emblem, the Guernica tree -- but to their own secret desire. In that new emotional and psychological context, female contact, the healing hands reaching out, constitute a rich and radical gesture of self-affirmation and, in my view, it becomes the common signature of these two films and of their gendered discourse. Another common signature, and a very important one, is Miró's and Lazcano's similar treatment of what Catherine Russell has called "narrative death" and its relation to the concept of closure.[10] In both films, the endings become a strong affirmation of an inner language that endures and transgresses the "social death" of both protagonists. Indeed, death figures largely in those endings which do not end but reopen the most vital tensions of the films'narratives. Thus, as Meri L. Clark has it:

> The 'true' death of which Carmen speaks is the closure of another element of the old narrative of her life, the narrative that had been interrupted with her rape. Carmen lives again "after" the rape -- a social death that re-opens the narrative. . . . The language that Carmen has been taught to speak throughout her life is an elaborate social construction that upholds a social order which commits violence against her. The infinite, silent space of the individual is the realm that Carmen actively seeks. . . . The conscious and incessant performance of death, the silencing of the performative language of violence, of life, is the only recourse to change, to hope for the future. Having found peace within herself and, to a certain extent, with the external world at the 'end' of El pájaro de la felicidad, Carmen at once crystallizes and reopens narratival possibilities: the future is that which has already been lived,

> she says, and peace is that which is found in death. (5-6)

Itziar's "peaceful death" has an identical value in Lazcano's Urte Ilunak. As the now adolescent Itziar lies down by the tree that harbors her hidden treasures, --the treasures of her imaginative self, of her privately "imagined community" in Anderson's formulation-- the very same tree where Itziar and Sofía became blood sisters, we hear the circular repetition of her own voice-over reciting these lines in a magical, incantatory tone:

> Si el tiempo, en sucesión única, no fuese tan injusto, llegaría hasta la niña que un día fuí y desnudaría, lentamente, el cuerpo que un día tuve, acariciándolo, luego, centímetro a centrímetro, hasta que aquellos ojos, tras los cuales un día miré, se cerrarán en el más dulce de los sueños. (If time, in its linear sucession, were not so unfair, I would go back to that girl that I once was and I would slowly undress that body that I once had, caressing it, then, inch by inch, till those eyes from which I once looked, would close in the sweetest of dreams).[11]

This "dream" is "the dark years", since film as dream imagery is the perfect vehicle to reimagine one's own past, to recreate one's own (national) identity or one's own "imagined community." Arantxa lazcano's poetic retracing of her historical time fulfills Itziar's impossible wish at the end of Urte Ilunak without providing any narrative closure to the crucial questions raised about the violent Basque society that brought her to the social death represented in the film's ending.

In bringing these two films together I hope to have shown how they articulate an alternative narrative desire for a beyond, for an ending to Spain's master narrative of Cainite violence. In their common gesture of reclaiming their protagonists' historical times and physical bodies, moreover, both Pilar Miró and Arantxa Lazcano have engendered new grounds in the representation of feminism and nationalism within and without the Spanish screen.

## Notes

[1]Unless otherwise indicated, all translations are mine.
[2] Consider, for instance, this paragraph: "The pivot of Saura's strategy lies in the fact that, from the very start, the protagonist, Antonio Cano, played brilliantly by José Luis López Vázquez, has been forced into a series of "therapeutic" dramatizations of key moments from his life, staged by his family in the hope of triggering the reawakening of his memory." (97) Or the following: "In these scenes of the re-created past, personal memory is grotesquely conflated with national history." (102) Ultimately, as Marvin D'Lugo has it, "what is at stake in *Garden of Delights* is the unmasking of the political relation of the spectator to history ." (104). I have also analyzed the importance of the amnesia motif as it is inscribed in the obsessive repetition of "family pictures," an attempt to fixate (oneself) (in) a present that denies any collective memory. See my "Paseo crítico e intertextual por el jardín edípico del cine español."
[3]I am referring to the notion of "national allegory" that Jameson first elaborated in his polemical "Third-World Literature in the Era of Multinational Capitalism." There he wrote that "the story of the private individual destiny is always an allegory of the embattled situation of the public third-world culture and society." (69). Later, Jameson developed the concept in his volume Signatures of the Visible, which is devoted to a critical reading of the"political unconscious" in contemporary cinema. Especially relevant to my discussion is the chapter entitled: "Class and Allegory in Contemporary Mass Culture" where the idea of "figurability" is presented.
[4]Marsha Kinder's "Micro and Macro Regionalism in "Vida en sombras" and Beyond" was first published in Cine-Lit. Essays on Peninsular Film and Fiction (131-146). Later it became chapter 8, "Micro- and Macro Regionalism in Catalan Cinema, European Coproductions and Global Television" in her volume: Blood Cinema. The Reconstruction of National Identity in Spain (388-441). Particularly relevant to my argument is the following paragraph: "Since regionality (like nationality) is an ideological construct, "regional film" and "regional television" are relativistic concepts. . . . Given this relativism, regionalism clearly may refer to geographic areas that are both "smaller" and "larger" than a nation. Thus, the terms "microregionalism" and "macroregionalism" help us to understand the regional/national/global interface." (388-9).

[5]Pilar Miró and Arantxa Lazcano were both very vocal and adamantly opposed to my own gendered approach to their films during the round table on "New Hispanic Cinema" that took place in March, 1994, in Portland, Oregon, during CINE-LIT-II, The Second International Conference on Hispanic Cinema and Literature.

[6]See my essay "Homoeroticism and Specular Transgression in Peninsular Feminine Narrative" where I elaborate on this new feminine/feminist aesthetic. See also Paul Julian Smith's Laws of Desire. Questions of Homosexuality in Spanish Writing and Film 1960-1990.

[7]I want to thank professor Donna Kerschner, whose question about the way Miró constructed visually her national allegory allowed me to realize the importance of the film's several "dissolves", and especially, of its most beautiful one. I am referring to the sequence in the Catalan Pyrinees, where the (im)permanence of the Francoist mother's and the conservative landowner father's narrative is "dissolved" in the final fade out that transports Carmen and the viewers from the soft green lights of the Pyrinees to the sun-drenched white and blue colors of the Andalusian South. North and South, (Catalan and Spanish), are not confused but "dissolved" in Pilar Miró's beautiful rendering of Carmen's inner resistance to dominant narratives.

[8]Pilar Miró was forced to resign from public office (General Director of Cinematography) because of a scandal involving accusations of having misappropriated public funds for private (clothing ) expenditures. The personal as political adopts here almost a paradoxical dimension.

[9]I am referring to my essay "La piedad profana de Pilar Miró", forthcoming in the Proceedings of CINE-LIT II, where I analyze her reversal of the traditional Christian figure.

[10]Quite relevant to my discussion of Pilar Miró's and Arantxa Lazcano's "undoing" of the social death of their protagonists is Catherine Russell's definition of narrative mortality, when she writes: "The term "narrative mortality" refers to the discourse of death in narrative film. It is a discourse produced by reading/viewing as much as it is by writing/filmmaking; it is both a critical method and a discursive practice. Narrative mortality is an "undoing" or "reading" of the ideological tendency of death as closure. It is a practice of resistance, with aspirations toward a radical politics of filmic narrativity. Narrative mortality is a method of understanding the function of narrative endings in the politics of representation, a means of moving beyond formalist

categories of "open" and "closed" endings, as well as mythic categories of fate and romance" (2).
[11]These lines are quoted directly from Arantxa Lazcano's original script: Urte Ilunak (The Dark Years). I thank Arantxa for her kindness in letting me have this unpublished document.

## Works Cited

Ackelsberg, Martha A. Free Women of Spain. Anarchism and the Struggle for The Emancipation of Women. Bloomington: Indiana Univ. Press, 1991.

Alonso de los Ríos, César. Si España cae... Asalto nacionalista al Estado. Madrid: Espasa Calpe, 1994.

Anderson, Benedict. Imagined Communities. Reflections on the Origin and Spread of Nationalism. London: Verso, 1983.

Bejarano, Fernando. "Arantxa Lazcano: 'Al comprobar que mucha gente aquí entiende la película he respirado.' Crónica del Festival de Montreal." Diario 16 (September 3, 1993): 39.

Cabello-Castellet, George, and Jaume Martí-Olivella, and Guy Wood, eds. Cine-Lit. Essays on Peninsular Film and Fiction. Corvallis: Oregon State Univ., 1992.

Clark, Meri L. "The Death of the Ending." Unpublished essay, 1995. 1-6.

D'Lugo, Marvin. The Films of Carlos Saura. The Practice of Seeing. Princeton: Princeton UP,

Hernández, Esteban. "Una historia local." El Mundo (October 22, 1993). E3.

Jameson, Fredric. "Third-World Literature in the Era of Multinational Capitalism." Social Text 15 (1986): 65-88.

- - - . Jameson. Fredric. Signatures of the Visible. New York: Routledge, 1990.

Kinder, Marsha. Blood Cinema. The Reconstruction of National Identity in Spain. Berkeley: Univ. of California Press, 1993.

Lazcano, Arantxa. "Urte Ilunak" (The Dark Years). Unpublished Original Script.

Llopart, Salvador. "Entrevista con Pilar Miró." La Vanguardia (May 6, 1993): 33.

Marinero, Francisco. "Demasiada poesía." El Mundo (October 29, 1993): E2.

Martí-Olivella, Jaume. "Homoeroticism and Specular Transgression in Peninsular Feminist Narrative." España Contemporánea 5.2 (Fall 1992): 17-25.

- - - . "Paseo crítico e intertextual por el jardín edípico del cine español." Letras Peninsulares (Spring 1994) V.7.1: 93-118.

- - - . "La Piedad profana de Pilar Miró." in the forthcoming Proceedings of CINE-LIT-II. Corvallis: Oregon State U, 1995.

Pérez-Millán, Juan Antonio. Pilar Miró. Directora de Cine. Madrid: SGAE, 1992.

Renan, Ernest. "Qu'est-ce qu'une nation?" Discours et Conférences. Paris: Calmann-Lévy, 1947: 277-310.

Rius, Felipe. "Urte Ilunak." *Egin* (September 17, 1993): 57.

Rubert de Ventós, Xavier. Nacionalismos. El laberinto de la identidad. Madrid: Espasa Calpe, 1994.

Russell, Catherine. Narrative Mortality. Death, Closure and New Wave Cinemas. Minneapolis: Univ. of Minnesota Press, 1995.

Smith, Paul Julian. Laws of Desire. Questions of Homosexuality in Spanish Writing and Film. 1960-1990. Oxford: Clarendon Press, 1992.

# Bigas Luna's Jamón Jamón: Remaking the National in Spanish Cinema

Marvin D'Lugo
Clark University

> Like signs, nations are constructs not of any external, referential world but of discourses.
> John Hartley[1]

## I. The Aesthetics of National Identity

For well over a decade, media historians and cultural theorists alike have been describing the process of cultural reconfiguration in European mass media that has come to defy the traditional boundaries of nation-states (Morely 34).[2] This displacement of traditional political boundaries by the patterns of diffusion of mass media has been called "cultural synchronization," described as "a canny reorientation of the national cultural industries in line with . . . the core of capitalistic production" (Maxwell 151). Inevitably, such realignments of audience have spawned a series of films that no longer respond to the assumed fixed nature of national cultures nor may be read in the context of immutable cultural identities. Rather, they are marked by a complex textual hybridity as well as a heterogeneity in the projection of their audience.

Bigas Luna's 1992 film, Jamón Jamón, is a striking self-conscious example of this phenomenon. Designed to circulate within the emerging "postmodern geography of Europe" (Morely 11), Jamón addresses its European spectatorship through a series of familiar cultural stereotypes while engaging its Spanish audience in often playful self-referential reflections on the process through which their identity as Spaniards has been reshaped by multinational capitalism. The film needs to be understood not only as evidence of a striking authorial style, but also as a highly creative response to the critical state of the Spanish film industry which, over recent decades, has lost a major part of its national audience (Hopewell 114-15) and thus finds itself forced to confront its relation to both national and transnational audiences.

It may well be this destabilization of the presumed audience of Spanish cinema that has led Bigas to situate Jamón in a semantic field implicitly shaped by the dynamics of micro- and macro-regionalism. According to Marsha Kinder, the Iberian experience of the micro- and macroregional phenomenon challenges the hegemony of Castilianized national culture by locating that culture within a regional/ national/ global interface that effectively reveals the relativistic nature and shifting centers involved in the formulation of cultural communities. Kinder argues that "because micro- and macroregionalism function codependently, fluidly shifting meaning according to context, they thereby serve as an effective means of both of asserting the subversive force of any marginal position and of destabilizing (or at least redefining) the hegemonic power of any center" (Kinder 389).

The result in the case of Jamón is a film that serves as a contestatory text, questioning the static forms of traditional Spanish culture while resemanticizing the representation of that culture around notions of multinational commodification. As Homi Bhabha observes, such a dynamics of shifting fictional centers and margins partakes of a postmodern sense of national cultures whose "implicit critique of the fixed and stable forms of the nationalist narrative makes it imperative to question those theories of the horizontal, homogeneous empty time of the nation's narrative" (Bhabha 303).

This dimension of the film's aesthetic and thematic conceptualization has been largely ignored by those critics and commentators who have only seen Jamón as a "sexy" Iberian narrative in the spirit of Almodóvar's cinema (Smith 138-9). Such accounts inevitably fail to note, however, the ways in which the film's visual style and narrative pointedly operate within a complex intertextual order developing patterns of address across the conventional boundaries of the nation. It is ultimately that aesthetic renegotiation of Spanishness that is at the center of Jamón as the film seeks to reposition its national and transnational audiences in relation to a radically reconfigured sense of national culture in Spain.

## II Allegorical Dimensions

Jamón's narrative is informed by a dialectical tension between a pristine sense of Spanish tradition and the entrepreneurial exploitation of that tradition. That tension is mirrored in the motivations of the film's principal characters, its formulation of narrative space, and, most conspicuously, its development of a series of exaggerated cultural symbols and motifs. Describing the inspiration for his conception of the film, Bigas writes: "El ordenador y el jamón conviven hoy en España, en una gran harmonía. Somos, posiblemente, uno de los pocos países donde el culto de lo animal y a la tecnología conviven." (The word processor and the ham coexist harmoniously today in Spain. We are possibly one of the few countries where the cult of the animal and technology coexist). The Catalan director further specifies the larger allegorical plan that shapes the development of characters, action, and setting: "dos jóvenes . . . el mar y la montaña, la costa y el interior, se disputan lo mejor del mundo . . . dos generaciones que se entrecruzan, los 70 y los 90 y entre dudas, disputas y peleas, llega Europea . . . Todo se pone al rojo vivo. Las sangres se calientan. Es el rapto de Europa, el triunfo del imperialismo europeo. (Two youths...the sea and the mountain, the coast and the interior, dispute the best things in the world...two generations cross paths, the seventies and the nineties, and between doubt, disputes, and fights, Europe enters the scene. Everything becomes red hot. Blood heats up. It's the kidnapping of Europe, the triumph of imperialism.) (Bigas Luna n. p. [3])

The full allegorical encryption of Bigas's script may not be entirely accessible to most audiences. Yet, undeniably, the exaggerated symbolic cast of the narrative does suggest that the textual elaboration of Jamón is being guided, as in allegory, by an extratextual symbolic system that parallels and mirrors the signifying system of the film.[4] That allegorical system takes shape from the start of the film with a shot of a detail from a billboard of the silhouette of the Osborne bull, the famous logo of a local brandy company that, during the 1960s and 1970s, dotted Spanish highways. Only retrospectively does the audience of Jamón recognize that the opening shots have been taken from a position just behind the bull's cojones, suggesting that the filmic narrative is symbolically framed by a mix of animal sexuality and brash commercialism.

The Osborne bull connects thematically with a series of traditional Spanish images that are also charged with symbolic significance. The most central of these relate to the culinary images of chorizo (sausage) and jamón (ham). Besides denoting types of meat, these terms have acquired certain sexual connotations in common parlance, referring to the predatory male or "stud" and the "slut" respectively, and become associated with the film's two central characters, Raúl and Silvia. To underscore the allegorical link of humans with food and sex, the male characters insist that female breasts have the taste of Spanish onion omelets with garlic. In this way, sexual desire is literally given a Spanish "flavor."

The recurrence of these food terms, as well as others, such as paella and roast suckling pig, becomes an expressive register through which the narrative deploys popular language to enunciate allegorical meanings. The essence of the struggle being enacted by the fictional chorizo and jamona is one that pits traditional Spanish popular culture, understood metaphorically by this culinary referent, against the economic development of European culture, conversely allegorized around pearls, women's shoes, and fancy cars. Ultimately, this is a story of economic transformation and its social consequences. For that reason Jamón privileges images, not only of food, but of other elements of popular culture as well, that reflect social and economic identities.

## III. Gender and Nation

This class-bound discourse and imagery enunciates what is, in effect, a dual narrative shaped by gendered polarities. From one perspective, Jamón may be read as the story of the Spanish male's self-deluding fantasy of his own sexual and social potency in an age of radical economic change. The centrality given to the male is eventually shown to be illusory in that it is the female who determines the signification of the male image and shapes the contexts within which the male lives out his illusion of power. A counter-narrative emerges drawing critical attention to female ascendendcy as articulated through the allegorical scenario shaped around two women, tellingly, two mothers: Conchita (Stefania Sandrelli) and Carmen (Ana Galiena). Carmen is a hostess in a roadside "putibar," the struggling mother of three daughters, the oldest of whom, Silvia (Penelope Cruz), works in the local underwear factory and is pregnant by the factory owner's son, José Luis (Jordi Molla). Conchita is the driving force behind the Sansón underwear factory and concocts a plan to break up her son's affair with Silvia. To this end, she enlists a local chorizo, Raúl, to seduce Silvia. But Conchita is herself so physically attracted to Raúl that she becomes, ironically, Silvia's double rival, both for José Luis and Raúl.

This intricate melodramatic narrative gradually reveals its allegorical underpinnings as pivotal cultural meanings accrue to each of the characters, most principally, the females. Carmen is identified with the more traditional icons of Spanish culture, especially the tortilla de patatas con cebolla, while Conchita is associated with the factory, business acumen, fancy shoes, and foreign cars. Though the plot that binds these two seemingly opposite figures together as fierce competitors appears to be about sexual attraction, their rivalry is really a symptomatic expression of the national struggle between traditional and contemporary definitions of economic culture.

In identifying the two mothers literally as a madre puta and a puta madre, as Bigas does in the film's final credit scroll, he is further extending the verbal-narrative play he began with the chorizo and jamona. Such characterizations emphasize just how inextricably tied sexual and economic identities are to the film's dramatic conflict. Indeed, besides their sexual identities, each mother represents a clearly defined position toward either traditional or European notions of economic order. Against this polarity, an intermediary position is embodied by Silvia. The young girl finds herself the object of a dramatic rivalry between José Luis and Raúl. Gradually, it becomes clear that Silvia is not just a pawn in the struggle of others but, as well, an actual rival, first with her own mother, with whom José Luis has also had sexual relations, then with Conchita, with whom she competes for Raúl's affections.

At the root of all of these rivalries is the essential point of Silvia's allegorical identity as the Spanish woman of the next generation, wooed by two males representing the traditionalist Iberian mentality of the interior and the commercial spirit that Bigas sees as linked with a coastal mentality. Her pairing first with José Luis and then with Raúl crystallizes the film's formulation of its cultural interrogation: the future direction of a society caught between its past and its future. Silvia finally appears aligned with a third figure, Manuel (Juan Diego), José Luis's ineffectual father who, according to Bigas, is the symbolic embodiment of European technocracy (Weinrichter 72).

Within this allegorical layering of the narrative, note should also be made of how the casting of actresses in the lead roles mirrors the thematic tension between the forces of Spanish and European economic identities. The appearance of Stenfania Sandrelli, a well-known Italian actress, in the role of Conchita not only helped initially to "sell" the film to a European market, but aligns her celebrity persona to her characterization of a Europeanized woman with a strong, independent sexual identity. Similarly, the casting of Penelope Cruz, a young Spanish actress, in the role of Silvia, reinforces her fictional identity as the youthful cipher of a promising new Spanish future. Thus, on both textual and extratextual levels, audiences are viewing a rivalry between generations, nationalities, and cultural outlooks.

## IV. A Vernacular Style

For all its elaborate allegorical density, Jamón Jamón should not be mistaken for a mere cerebral game of decipherment addressed to a small intellectual audience. Essential to the film's enunciation is its construction of a vernacular style, that is, one that appropriates, even flaunts, elements of Spanish popular culture, reducing them to the lingua franca of cliches and caricatures that beguile foreign tourists, while using these as a short hand through which to address a national audience. We have already noted how the sexual characterization of Raúl and Silvia as chorizo and jamona, for instance, coincides with popular foreign stereotypes of oversexed Spaniards. On another level, Jamón cleverly deploys a rich Spanish visual tradition in order to evoke a more "artistic" textual identification with Spain through the figures of Goya, Dalí, and Buñuel.[5] Yet such an identification, far from distancing audiences from the film by esoteric cultural allusions, actually works in the opposite way by reinforcing the non-Spaniard's impression that this is a story involved in some generic way with a broadly-defined Spanish national culture.

The Buñuelian intertext, for instance, is more of a parody of the Spanish Surrealist master than a homage. In a brief dream sequence Silvia's emotional predicament is restaged with a barrage of Freudian symbols, adding what appears to be a dimension of pop psychologism to her character thus reaffirming the film's overall vernacular style.

A more significant artistic allusion is the series of motives associated with Dalí's Naturaleza viva y muerta that has become an almost axiomatic element of the visual style of Bigas's films over the past decade and a half (Espelt 71). This intertext is apparent in Bigas's various efforts to blur the textual lines between living and inanimate objects, in effect, to "object-ify" certain characters, so that they embody the underlying entrepreneurial belief that individuals are mere objects and can be bought and sold. From the very opening images of the film, this ubiquitous commercial spirit serves to transform the human figure into the fetishized object of commercial exploitation.

The narrative and visual insistence on culture commodified underscores Bigas's underlying conception of post-Franco Spain as it shifts from a paradigm of traditional culture to one of technological multinational "business." To this end the film draws the audience's attention to a series of images that reduce cultural archetypes to sexual cliches and treat them in ways that are reminiscent of the paintings of Andy Warhol. The point of this treatment is, as in Warhol, not simply the image as an end in itself, but as a product, thereby foregrounding the process through which cultural icons have been refigured for commercial exploitation (Hughes 351).

Far from weighing the film down with a heavy aesthetization of action and image, this intertextual visual style connects pointedly with the theme of cultural commercialization by linking spectatorship itself to the commercial enterprise. We may readily note this in the proliferation of billboards as well as in the frequent slow pan shots used in the film. Such touches, inspired by a variety of commercial media, lead the audience to "scan" rather than to read the film. Thus the specular activity elaborated throughout Jamón may be understood as a mirroring of the world of publicity, commercialism and commodification of which Dalí and Warhol appear to be inspirational divinities.

To illustrate exactly how this complex relay of allegorical narrative and vernacular cinematic style operates on the level of textual practice, I will focus on two key sequences: the credits and opening scenes as they lay out in very explicit and succinct terms the logic of this transformation of Spanish culture, and the final scene of Jamón in which this thematic is reformulated as an interrogation for a contemporary Spanish audience. In particular, I want to draw attention to the way within Bigas's own stylistic formation that the image generates the narrative and thematic axis of the film and thus facilitates a kind of comprehension that is both direct and "easily accessible" to foreign as well as national audiences.

## V. Commercial Overtures

The dazzling opening sequence enunciates a series of critical messages that transcend the usual verbal/narrative formulation of sound cinema and become easily legible between and among various cultural communities. The credits are shot in red and white letters against a grainy black screen as the soft background music of the film's musical theme is heard. Gradually, we discern a camera movement downward at the end of the credits along with the emerging sound of trucks or other vehicles on a highway. There is also a noticeable squeaking sound that slowly gains force over the music. The steady downward tracking eventually reveals the camera situated in a position behind what will be identified in a subsequent shot as one of the enormous billboard silhouettes of the Osborne bull. The squeaking, as we shortly discover, is, in fact, the flapping of the testicles which are about to come loose from the billboard.

The silhouetted bull, an image of traditional Spain that goes back to the españoladas, those inventions of Spanishness first formulated by the French and gradually absorbed by Spaniards, announces boldly the commodification of a certain historical notion of Spanishness as the central theme of the film. Bigas's camera view of the highway from a site between the bull's legs underscores that sense of the commercial framed by the sexual/ cultural icon. At the same time, it shows the discrepancy between the static forms of the past and the movement that is engendered by contemporary commerce.

Enhancing the commercialization of culture is the monochromatic nature of the image, a distinctive icon that lends itself to facile reproduction and packaging. With the figuration of this marketable cultural motif, we are immediately thrown into a world in which the formula of expression is Warholesque. The Osborne bull becomes a Spanish variant of the Campbell's soup can: an infinitely reproducible two-dimensional surface image that embodies a broader culture of commerce. The shot of the bull's silhouette ends abruptly with a rapid cut to a horizontal tracking across an arid and parched terrain until we come upon a space where Raúl is seen first at a distance, then in medium close-up, practicing torero moves with a carretón, a mechanical bull on a unicycle, pushed by a companion. The scene cuts from an establishing shot to a close-up of Raúl's crotch and buttocks emphasizing the pale blue of his shorts which contrasts with the earlier blackness of the Osborne bull. A few unintelligible grunting sounds from the two men are heard.

The image of Raúl practicing his bullfighting moves is another variation of the bull icon. This one, though, holds a particular social meaning for Spaniards in that it captures in a visual tableau the scenario of social ascent that has been a commonplace in Spanish culture for nearly a century: the idea that the corrida represents for Spain's marginalized southern rural males access to rapid social and economic success. While exploiting the static, atemporal iconography of Spanishness, which makes it so easily legible to foreigners, Bigas continually fixes as the back-story to his mythic narrative Spaniards' struggle for economic improvement.

Textually, the shift of scenes is significant in that it substitutes the close-up of the bull's testicles with the close-up of Raúl's crotch, thereby giving emphasis to the conflation of inanimate and live figures. Rhetorically, the logic of the shift is metaphoric, that is, a series of visual substitutions. The effectiveness of the visual metaphor as Bigas uses it is not only based on an economy of expression but also on an innate transparency of metaphoric meanings. One thing literally replaces another both in the textual formulation of the narrative as well as in the social world described by that narrative. The cut from Raúl's training to the first shot of an anonymous young woman on the production line at the Sansón factory, for instance, is by way of establishing the displacement of traditional male economic and sexual power by that of the female.

After shots of the female worker, the camera cuts to another place in the factory where a women in a man-tailored suit is being followed by a group of men. This is Conchita, the owner of the Sansón factory, who is arguing with her executives. Significantly, the first audible words of dialogue in the film are spoken by Conchita and underscore the film's narrative thematic:

"No olvides que son las mujeres que compran los calzoncillos a los hombres y un buen paquete vende (Don't forget that it's women who buy underwear for men and a good bulge sells!). Conchita not only voices an economic fact but affirms, as well, the position of power that the female has come to assume in modernizing Spain.

Her appearance serves as a bridge between the assembly line of women who have replaced men as the source of economic power to a new line-up, this one of young men in bikini briefs being interviewed and videotaped in what is apparently an audition for a men's underwear ad. This regendered "chorus line" is presented in a three-shot sequence: first an establishing shot that situates the men being interviewed as the video camera scans from each man's crotch to his face; then a close-up of Raúl reciting his name, age, and occupation; finally the image of a television monitor positioned in a room adjoining the audition space, where Conchita reappears viewing Raúl's "audition."

This male assembly line, an obvious parody of the traditional phallocentric placement of women as the object of a male glance, reiterates the displacement of men within the visual and social economies of contemporary Spain. The sequence further emphasizes meanings that have thus far been constructed: Raúl's crotch in close-up defines the Iberian male as his sexual image, literally his "paquete." Only secondarily does he have a name, an age, an occupation. That he should work for a meat packer named "Los Conquistadores" merely reinforces the notion of commodifying historical culture as product while replicating phallic imagery. Eventually, this very torso will appear on a billboard replacing the Osborne bull as the symbol of a new Spanish commercial spirit.

Throughout the entire opening sequence, camera movement is continually equated with billboard "scanning" in order to stress the conflation of specularization with commerce. The movement from phallocentric iconography to Conchita's private television monitoring of Raúl's audition foretells the cultural logic through which Spanish social and economic power is now seen as driven by the female. It is no coincidence that the name Bigas gives to the brand of men's underwear being promoted is Sansón, evoking a mythic antecedent to the ensuing narrative of female displacement of male power (Kinder 221). By means of such ostentatious rewritings of the codes of traditional cultural representation, Jamón constructs a series of positions from which the act of seeing is charged with a cluster of critical social and cultural meanings.

## VI. The Duel with Cudgels

The credit and prologue sequence establish the patterns of tension and potential conflict that result from the economic and social refiguration of Spain, setting the stage for the intricate generational melodrama that ensues around the figures of Silvia and Raúl. That melodrama reaches its climax in the final scene, the confrontation between José Luis and Raúl as they battle each other in what amounts to the allegorical duel between cultural and economic mentalities. The action of that sequence takes place in and around the ham warehouse where Raúl both works and lives. This is the site to which Conchita has pursued Raúl and where the two now make love. José Luis breaks in and attacks Raúl with a ham leg. To defend himself, Raúl grabs another, larger ham leg and the youths quickly move to the dusty yard in front of the warehouse overlooking the rugged landscape.

The duel that follows is a conspicuous restaging of Goya's painting, Duelo a garrotazos, earlier dramatized in a scene from Saura's 1963 film, Llanto por un bandido (D'Lugo 50). The painterly treatment given to the scene serves to emphasize the symbolically charged nature of the duel and to entice the audience into a more active engagement in the process of allegorical decipherment in the final moments of the film. Like the opening sequence, this tragic finale underscore essential qualities of Bigas's allegorical style as it inscribes a series of new meanings for the viewer to decipher around a set of striking images.

As the final scene begins, Raúl's fatal blow to José Luis's head appears to have resolved the seething emotional and social conflict in favor of the resurgent power of a primitive violence. But instead of stabilizing this impression by bringing the film to a simple and rapid closure, Bigas adds a brief tableau vivant in which the six principal characters of the film regroup in pairs further reinforcing an allegorical logic that seems to transcend the merely melodramatic story.

That tableau begins to take form just after Raúl strikes the blow that kills José Luis, and Manuel arrives in his shiny Mercedes Benz car, accompanied by Silvia, who has brought him to help prevent this very duel. When Raúl becomes aware of

Silvia in the car with Manuel, he is enraged and batters the front of the Mercedes with the ham leg, then falls prostrate to the ground. Manuel and Silvia get out of the car and approach José Luis's body. Silvia, bending over the fallen body, holds the dead youth's hand and we see in close-up their intertwined hands with José Luis's Rolex watch gleaming in sharp contrast to the Coke can cap wedding band he had earlier given Silvia as a token of his love. These course commercial images restate the class tensions that have, in a sense, led the characters to this tragic impasse in the narrative.

As the character huddle around the body, Carmen arrives on her scooter. Like Silvia, she has rushed here in a futile attempt to thwart José Luis's murderous attack. With Carmen's arrival, Manuel and Silvia recede from the site of the body and stand immobile in an embrace that seems to confuse shared bereavement at the death of their lover and son with erotic desire. Carmen approaches Conchita who is now holding her son in a classic pietà position. The camera tracks to reveal a new formation in which Raúl is seen kneeling in a penitent position at Conchita's side as she passes José Luis's body to Carmen who now resumes the pietà posture. In its totality, this new regrouping suggests José Luis's quasi-religious status as a martyr to the forces of primitive violence embodied by Raúl.

A cut to the clouds above marks the beginning of final continuous camera movement of the film as it scans the six principals in these curious new groupings. That camera movement begins with the slightly distanced image of Manuel and Silvia, in an immobile embrace as they look on at the scene, then a gradual movement toward the other two couples: Conchita consoling Raúl and Carmen embracing José Luis's body. Of the three couples perhaps the most startling image is that of Manuel and Silvia as it poses a bitterly ironic commentary on the earlier dramatic struggle between José Luis and Raúl. The pairing of the Euro-executive, Manuel, and the humble factory worker, Silvia, suggests a new formulation of the Spanish family, one forged from the very antagonisms that earlier defined the community. The implication seems to be that the future for Spain will be a troubled marriage, born of the union of the two extremes symbolized by Manuel and Silvia, and yet somehow expressing a hybridization of those oppositions to be embodied ultimately in José Luis's child, which Silvia is carrying.

The off-screen refrain of a popular love song is now heard as the camera cuts to a long-shot of the characters standing motionless against the setting sun. In the distance a slight cloud of dust is seen rising from the road. The sound of cattle bells which have been growing louder throughout the scene is now heard more clearly as the lingering shot reveals the approach of a shepherd and his flock. The soundtrack during these final moments of the film mixes a contemporary love ballad with sheep bells, thus rhyming with the credit sequence in which a musical theme was also mixed with the distanced sound of modern highway traffic. This auditory and visual pastiche underscores the pattern of radical shifting images and styles that has characterized much of Jamón from the very start. The momentary triumph of Raúl's primitive machismo over the more enlightened tradition of the coast was mitigated by the glaring image of Manuel and Silvia paired, only to have that simplistic reading of the allegory further destabilized by the cloud of dust from the shepherd's flock that will soon envelope the scene.

The underlying aesthetic concept that informs this progression, as it does throughout the film, is the basic rejection of the static and largely reified notions of culture, especially as these have served to fix social meanings for individuals and communities. Bigas's dialogical theme, reflected in the visual intertexts as well as in the allegorized characters, has worked to destabilize the viewers' sense of a simplistic and immobile tableau. Thus, the notion of narrative closure with the triumph of a simple past or an equally simple future is continually thwarted by opposing elements that suggest to contemporary audiences the dynamic and continually changing nature of Spanish culture. Bigas's insistent juxtapositioning of visual styles and characters is really by way of an enticement for that audience to respond to the challenge of a culture in the throes of redefining itself in the world by continually renegotiating its sense of its past and future.

Notes

[1]"Invisible Fictions: Television Audiences, Paedocracy, Pleasure," in Television Studies: Textual Analyses, edited by Gary Burns

and Robert J. Thompson. New York: Praeger, 1989). As cited in Kinder, 388.

[2]The process, though largely defined in the context of television, also has important relevance to cinema. See especially discussions by Kinder, 388-447 and Hopewell.

[3] That allegorical code is further detailed in the symbolic choice of vehicles, such as the European Mercedes that tempts the film's heroine, Silvia. For a detailed discussion of this allegorical decipherment, see Weinrichter, 72.

[4] In considering the loose application of the term allegory to film criticism, David Bordwell reminds us of the rigorous definition of the term: "in a narrower sense, allegory is a type of holistic enactment in which the trajectory of this text is interpreted as being congruent with that of some other text, or with the categories or precepts of a preexisting doctrine" (Bordwell 195). Given Bigas's efforts to construct a narrative that mirrors in detail the contemporary status of Spain's economic alignment with multinational capitalism, the description of the film as an allegory seems especially justified.

[5] It is interesting to observe that Ramón Espelt, writing some seven years before the release of Jamón, identified Buñuel, Dalí and Goya as principal sources of the visual structure of Bigas's work, especially in terms of the centrality of the image. See Espelt 70-71.

## Works Cited

Bhabha, Homi K. "DissemiNation: Time, Narrative and the Margins of the Modern Nation," Nation and Narration. London and New York: Routledge, 1991, 290-322.

Bigas Luna. "Notas sobre el proyecto de Bigas Luna." Pressbook Jamón Jamón n. p.

Bordwell, David. Making Meaning: Inference and Rhetoric in the Interpretation of Cinema. Cambridge, MA: Harvard University Press, 1989.

D'Lugo, Marvin. The Films of Carlos Saura: The Practice of Seeing. Princeton, N. J., Princeton University Press, 1991.

Ramón Espelt. Mirada al Món de Bigas Luna. Barcelona: Editorial Laertes, 1989.

Hopewell, John. "Art and a Lack of Money: The Crises of the Spanish Film Industry," Quarterly Review of Film and Video 13.4 (1991): 113-22.

Robert Hughes. The Shock of the New. New York: Alfred A Knopf, 1981.

Marsha Kinder. Blood Cinema: The Reconstruction of National Identity in Spain. Berkeley: University of California Press, 1993.

Maxwell, Richard. The Spectacle of the Nation: Spanish Television, Nationalism, and Political Transition. Minneapolis, University of Minnesota Press, 1995.

Morley, David and Kevin Robbins, "Spaces of Identity: Communications Technologies and the Reconfiguration of Europe," Screen 26.1 (January/February, 1985): 10-34.

Smith, Paul Julian. Desire Unlimited: The Cinema of Pedro Almodóvar. London: Verso, 1994.

Weinrichter, Antonio. La línea del vientre: el cine de Bigas Luna Gijón, Festival del cine de Gijón, 1992.

## Kika: Vision Machine

Paul Julian Smith
University of Cambridge

One photograph; three captions. The photograph: Pedro Almodóvar peeking out from between scarlet curtains, a green spotted bow in his black curly hair. The captions: "Genius or hype?" (El País Semanal, Madrid);[1] "Ready for our closeup?" (Out, New York);[2] "I feel like a carnival freak" (Observer, London).[3] This publicity shot for Kika recapitulates the three issues which, I have argued, are fundamental for any understanding of the cinema of Pedro Almodóvar.[4] The very visible bow is the sign of a conspicuous visual pleasure coded as feminine in film theory. The polka dots or lunares on the bow and curtains function as a parodic pointer to Spanishness, to the españolada.[5] Finally, the adoption by a man of this flamboyant femininity serves as an index of homosexuality, defined here not as desire for the same sex, but as identification with the other.[6] Beyond these references to gender, nationality, and homosexuality, however, the photograph is framed by the captions which give evidence of the audiences by which Kika was received. The Spanish caption testifies to the continuing debate over the artistic value of the nation"s most commercially successful filmmaker. The North American invites a metropolitan gay readership to recognize itself in a camp quotation.[7] Finally, the British objectifies the filmmaker, confining him and his work to an exotic and eccentric space from which the UK general public is safely insulated.

Problematization, identification, objectification: the different press framings of a single image remind us that the social reception of cinema cannot be dissociated from the work itself, that the tributary media serve actively to produce a multiplicity of audiences for a filmic work. More importantly, perhaps, the publicity shot suggests an instantaneous redoubling or con/fusion of presentation and representation typical of Almodóvar's cinema. Simultaneously director and actor, Almodóvar presides over a proliferating series of discrete images typified by the grid on the film's poster, in which each actor is isolated in a repeated pattern of high definition fluorescent colour shot against a white background. Once more the graphic style (by long time collaborator Juan Gatti) con/fuses presentation and representation: contact sheet format publicity material (captioned by Out "Pedro's People") extends the aesthetics of the film itself to members of the production company and others who have contributed to Almodóvar"s career over the last decade. In this parade of phatic images, whose purpose is simply to "force [the viewer] to look, to hold his or her attention",[8] designer, actor, make up artist, and publicity person, each is indistinguishable from the other.

This triumph of design in Almodóvar is hardly news. What I will suggest in this paper, however, is that the logic or paralogic of the publicity shot is symptomatic of what French cultural theorist Paul Virilio has called "the vision machine", a regime of ever increasing visibility which leads, paradoxically, to an aesthetics of disappearance or of blindness, which is "the result of an ever brighter illumination, of the intensity of definition" (Vision 14). At the opening party for Kika in London, an event dense with fashionable trade marks (from the locale itself to the free food and drink served in the VIP section) Almodóvar was accompanied by models dressed in the Jean Paul Gaultier costumes worn by Victoria Abril's character in the film.[9] The costumes, subsequently auctioned for an AIDS charity, thus substituted for the bodies of the actors who had worn them. There could be no more transparent emblem of what Virilio has called the "disidentified image", a certain "waning of reality" produced by the "instrumental splitting of modes of perception and representation" (49). But that "passage from vision to visualization" (13) exemplified by Almodóvar's fashion conscious identity parades is also, and quite explicitly, the object of critique within Kika. And as in Virilio's The Vision Machine, in Kika the con/fusion of presentation and representation (the shift from the dialectical duration to the paradoxical instant) is related to the decline of cinema and the rise of video. Let us, then, suspend the questions of audience and reception to which I referred above and of which I have written elsewhere,[10] and take seriously the critique of reproductive technology we find in Kika, reading it not as a topical intervention in the debate on Spanish media in the 90s (although clearly it is), but rather as a comment on and a symptom of that depersonalization of vision and duplication of the body which follows in the wake of the vision machine.[11]

Kika's credit sequence begins with a keyhole, a camera shutter, and a woman undressing. On a shoot for a lingerie spread, mother obsessed photographer Ramón (Alex Casanovas) pleads with his model to exhibit "authentic" sexual pleasure for the lens. It is, however, Ramón whose pleasure must always be mediated by visual prosthesis. Fumbling with voyeuristic delight over the bored model's body, he represents that distancing teletopology, which for Virilio "anticipates human movement, outstripping every displacement of the body" (6). Once "the visual field is reduced to that of a sighting device" (13) (a process which the cinema audience is invited to share), then the subject is absent from the scene of his sight: contradicting the reality principle that "Everything I see is . . . within my reach"(7), the reality effect of the new logistics of perception abstracts the body of the witness, "delocalizing geometrical optics" (12): a later shot in the sequence reveals that the model is not, as we had thought, lying supine on a bed, but is rather standing against a vertical mock up.

Kika's temporal frame is as disorientating as its spatial optic. Flashing forward from the opening time frame in which Ramón discovers his mother's supposed suicide to the present in which Kika addresses her cosmetics class on the glory of the false eyelash, the plot immediately flashes back once more to the televised book promotion in which Nicholas (Peter Coyote) plugs his autobiographical novel on a show presented (or, as she puts it, "represented") by Almodóvar's own mother Francisca Caballero; and to Kika's inadvertent resurrection of the narcoleptic Ramón, as she attempts to "give back natural colour" to a corpse. While the TV show juxtaposes a parodically heightened regionalism (Manchegan mise en scene) with the delocalized modernity and internationalism of a US author (and actor, dubbed by a Spaniard), the resurrection scene also laments the loss of a social or familial sphere in the supposed "Americanization" of a solitary wake without family or friends. If here the cosmetic is indistinguishable from the organic (is Ramón's flush natural or artificial?), then Ramón's narcolepsis, the con/fusion of life and death, is also the inversion of an order of perception: the close up of his blank, unseeing look signals a new sightless vision in an age when "objects perceive us" (59), when, in Virilio's words "the human eye no longer gives signs of recognition, no longer organises the search for truth" (43).

Nicholas's subsequent arrival at the sterile new Atocha station also hints at this "topographical amnesia" in which the body's lived relation to a duration of space and sight is lost. But Virilio's "permanent regime of bedazzlement", his intuition that "the most distinctive cities [in this case Madrid] bear within them the capacity of being nowhere" (10), is most spectacularly born out by the sequences taken from the real-life crime show "The Worst of the Day", hosted by Victoria Abril's Andrea Caracortada. Here Gaultier's celebrated costumes pose or expose the supplementary status of the body in the vision machine: in the first, exploding prosthetic breasts pierce the skin tight surface of a black gown, dappled with plastic blood; in the second, body parts (eyes, ears, breasts) are redoubled by electronic prostheses (video, audio, lighting) fused with a black rubber epidermis. As substitute for the body's waning powers and addition to traditional human faculties, the costumes parade that instrumentalization of the senses that Virilio both laments and celebrates. It is an instrumentalization reinforced by Almodóvar's (or Alfredo Mayo's)[12] shooting style. Thus Andrea's video footage of everyday horrors (the on camera murder of a mother in a cemetery) is offered to us from the ambiguous point of view, at once objective and subjective, of the cyborg camera costume. And wilfully con/fusing presentation and representation Andrea is (like Almodóvar in the broader spectacle of his cinema) at once actor and director of her horror shows, playing a conspicuous role in them even as she insists she simply reproduces them, mechanically, for the screen. The communal space of a live audience (here reduced to phantasmal empty seats) is displaced by the fragmented electronic audience, the public space by the public image: Andrea delivers one homily while seated on a TV set; Rossy de Palma's maid is shot from behind the screen which, in a symptomatic reversal, appears to be watching her. Caught by and in the video frame, bodies no longer inhabit the universe; rather the (electronic) universe inhabits them (27).

But Virilio would argue that this "perception of special detachment", this "integrated circuit of vision" and death (38) is not simply the result of technological development or deployment. Rather Andrea's Medusa-look (which dispossesses, blinds, immobilizes) is the terror-effect which is the dark shadow of rationality and Enlightenment. The reality show merely mimics that "illumination of the private sphere", that desire "to obtain a total image of society by dispersing its dark secrets" (34) deployed by modern governmentality; tracking down darkness, it exhibits both an "obsession with the unsaid" which demands witnesses be called on to confess and a "totalitarian desire for clarification" (34), which demands images be exhibited to the greatest number of citizens. Andrea's advantage however, is that video permits her a certain compression of time associated with its visual instantaneity (37). It is Virilio's argument (and one confirmed by Kika) that when image redoubles object and time space then there must be a crisis in media characterized by delay and representation such as cinema to the advantage of media devoted to the instant of presentation such as video. Although Andrea's same day reportages are not real time, they point to the displacement of past, present, and future by a new temporal order of real time and delayed time, of an endlessly repeatable and continuously pending "latent immediacy" (43).

Two later scenes exemplify the new temporal order of the vision machine. First, when Ramón and Kika attempt unsuccessfully to make love, the former insists on using a polaroid camera as a "sight line" for his desire, thus bypassing the body. Through a technological "phenomenon of acceleration" (4), Ramón reduplicates the instant, privileging "precision of detail" over that "sharing of duration" necessary for any intersubjective experience. As Rodin said of a photographic model, Ramón is like a "man suddenly struck with paralysis", his sense of "felt temporality" lost to the "image-time-freeze" (2) of the photographer who, unlike the sculptor or painter does not "take his body with him" (16). Secondly, and more notoriously, Kika is raped by escaped porno actor Paul Bazzo ("polvazo" = "Big Fuck"), a character unable to distinguish between a fictional and an authentic sexual performance, and her violation is replayed on a video submitted by a mysterious voyeur to Andrea's TV show. Here once more, according to the paradoxical logic of video, a means of action is immediately a means of representation (29). And once more, it is a question of detail here. Virilio cites sarcastically Benjamin's proposal that photography "opens up the clear field where all intimacy leads to the clarification of details" (23). The voyeur's attachment to the intensive detail is thus not simply a psychic mechanism; rather it is a technique typical of a society of surveillance: "the elucidation of details [is a] means of governing, [a form of] omnivoyance" (33). It is an omnivoyance characterized by a redoubling of the point of view. In just the same way our initial "objective" viewpoint of the rape is first subjectivized by the revelation that Ramón had been the voyeur who notified the singularly ineffective police only to be objectivized once more by Andrea's confirmation that the videotape was sent to her by one of her multiple and anonymous voyeuristic collaborators. This is for Virilio precisely the definition of the vision machine: a form of sightless vision or automated perception in which viewpoints are split and perception shared "between the animate (the living subject) and the inanimate (the object, the seeing machine)" (59). Kika's unknown witness, whose identity and location Almodóvar does not care to elucidate, embodies that depersonalization and delocalization typical of the paradoxical logic of the video era.

The last reel of the film repeats, once more, the redoubling of the look which is also the con/fusion of presentation and representation: Nicholas reveals he is a serial killer to Andrea and to her camera simultaneously; as he lies dying he offers his fictional manuscript to Kika, assuring her that it will be an autobiographical bestseller; and when, after multiple murders, Kika exclaims: "How long will this nightmare last?" she echoes a question members of the cinema audience may well be asking themselves. Struggling ever more desperately to bring the body into visibility (displaying repeated frontal nude shots of Bibi Andersen), Almodóvar exhausts his image repertoire, surrendering to the intensity of the phatic image rather than the scope or space of the public image, proving that when truth is no longer masked but rather eclipsed by its televized image, "what is perceived is already finished" (69), evacuated by its own luminous velocity.

It is Virilio's contention that the formal logic of eighteenth century painting or engraving gave way to the dialectical logic of nineteenth century photography or film, to be displaced itself by the paradoxical logic of video or computer graphics. It is a shift from the real, to the actual, to the virtual similar to those traced by other theorists such as Baudrillard. However, Virilio's account of the "crisis in traditional forms of public representation" suggests that Kika is at once a critique and a symptom of the shift from film to video. The supposed "disaster" of the film (much trumpeted by Spanish critics) thus goes beyond Kika's own undeniable narrative incoherence[13] to speak of the problems of affect, politics, and a critical space in the age of the vision machine. Let us begin with affect. For Virilio, the "hyperrealism" of surveillance procedures (including the law and police) has led to the devaluation of eyewitness accounts and a putting to death of the body: "How", he asks, "can we hope to scandalize, surprise, move to tears before . . . the distant technological outcome of the merciless more light of revolutionary terror?" (44). It is a question burlesqued by Almodóvar himself when he has Andrea warn her audiences that her programme may offend their sensibilities, if they have any left. But it is also a question to be posed to an Almodóvar whose quest to illuminate the bizarre and the novel has now been outstripped by the mainstream TV shows he affects to despise.[14] In a cinema, such as Almodóvar's, in which sensation was always crosscut with sentiment, this exhaustion of affect may prove lethal indeed. The increasingly cursory nature of Kika's detective story (a genre which Virilio associates with the "instrumentalization of the photographic image" [36]) also bears witness to the decline of narrative in the age of instant video testimony.

The second problem is that of politics. Virilio claims that the temporal mode of film documentaries was that of the "fatum" or event completed-in-the-past: "They . . . induced a feeling of the irreparable, and through a dialectical reaction, fostered [the] violent will to engage the future" (25). The instantaneity of video, however, in which the "presence of the past is [no longer] impressed on plate or film" (64), produces not events but accidents; and its paralogic, outstripping and displacing the felt duration of history, can engender at most a momentary surprise in its mesmerized audience. Kika both laments that loss and compulsively repeats it in its neglect of duration or suspense (the police investigation is derisory) and its scorn for psychological depth or motivation (Nicholas's malevolence is unexplained). An unlikely moraliser, Almodóvar can only lay bare the ethical paralysis wrought by the video spectacle; he cannot propose any singular and completed event (certainly not the mediatized rape) which might provoke in his audience the potential for political engagement inspired by the cinema of the past.

Finally there is the question of a critical space. I have argued that Kika displays that depersonalized and delocalized perception typical of the phatic image which prizes intensity over extension, immediacy over topographical memory. Virilio goes beyond this, however, arguing that the instrumentalization of vision since photography has radically transformed personal and public perceptions of space and time, citing:

> [the] exhaustion of the Cartesian tradition which had sprung out of the original invention of the serialization not only of forms-images but also of mental images and which was the origin of the City and human social communities based on the constitution of collective paramnesias, on the

> 'ideal of a world essentially the same, essentially shared as that preliminary foundation of the construction of meaning we call geometry'[15]. (27)

Lamenting the loss of the collectivity, both psychic and social, deploring the loss of the City, as a place of imaginary continuity and sameness, Kika also reproduces uncritically those losses in its celebration of the unmotivated and dislocated, in its vindication of singularity and surprise. Almodóvar thus privileges speed over space, image over object, costume over body. In the final sequence, neglecting her responsibilities towards the revived Ramón, Kika heads off with a handsome stranger on a new adventure. And the camera tilts down for a final shot of the white line down the centre of the road she is travelling. It is typical of a narrative in which, for all its references to contemporary Madrid, "the strategic value of speed's 'no-place' has definitively outstripped the value of place" (31) and "seeing the world becomes not only a matter of spatial difference but . . . a matter of speed, of acceleration or deceleration" (21).

Now territorial space has been devalued (now Kika has no home to return to), we are lost in the vision machine with Almodóvar; and we may, like his heroine, feel we have lost our way. But Kika's "failure" admits no simple solution and is not accidental or singular; rather it points, with characteristic perversity, to a pervasive exhaustion of cinema, one which (for Virilio) can neither be surmounted, nor circumvented. The seeing devices which dispense with the body; the permanence of the "regime of bedazzlement"; the madness and terror which are the fellow travellers of technology (16, 10, 29); it is enough that Almodóvar should raise such questions; we can hardly expect him to solve them.

## Notes

[1] 19 October 1993.
[2] May 1994.
[3] 5 June 1994.
[4] See my Desire Unlimited: The Cinema of Pedro Almodóvar (London: Verso, 1994).

[5] For a lavishly illustrated tribute to and record of the españolada see Terenci Moix, Suspiros de España: la copla y el cine de nuestro recuerdo (Barcelona: Plaza y Janés, 1993). Camp icons from Concha Piquer to Concha Velasco are shown here in polka-dotted frocks.
[6] For a recent critical account of homosexuality as identification with the opposite sex see Mandy Merck, "The Train of Thought in Freud's 'Case of Homosexuality in a Woman'", in the same author's collection of essays Perversions: Deviant Readings (London: Virago, 1993), pp. 13-32.
[7] The quote is, of course, from Billy Wilder's Sunset Boulevard (1950). Compare the ironic caption to a cover shot of a wide eyed and open mouthed Almodóvar in the British gay glossy Attitude: "Outrageous!" (July 1994). In spite of Almodóvar's continuing disavowal of a gay audience for his films, Kika benefited from copious and favourable coverage in the UK gay press.
[8] This is my first citation from Paul Virilio, The Vision Machine (London: BFI); French original, La Machine de vision (Paris: Galilée, 1988). Virilio is known above all as the theorist of the reciprocal relation between reproductive technologies and war; see War and Cinema: The Logistics of Perception (London: Verso, 1989; French original, 1984).
[9] To cite the press release (Mark Borkowski, 9 June 1994): "On Thursday June 30th at 8.00 pm the coolest of London's hot-spots The Fridge plays host to superstyle stars of fashion and film in a night of fund-raising for Europe's leading HIV and AIDS centre, London Lighthouse." This was the first time that Almodóvar had attempted to reproduce in London the lavish parties created in Madrid for the openings of his films.
[10] "Future Chic", Sight and Sound (January 1994), pp. 6-10.
[11] Rarely credited with any serious concerns in Spain, Almodóvar is regularly attributed intellectual ambitions in France; see Frédéric Strauss's location report "The Almodóvar Picture Show", Cahiers du Cinéma 471 (September 1993): 34-42; and the same author's interview with the director on Kika in Pedro Almodovar [sic]: conversations avec Frédéric Strauss (Paris: Cahiers du Cinéma, 1994): 124-148. Strauss reproduces collages and draft designs by Dis Berlín which confirm the fusion of the organic (flowers, animals, women's bodies) and the technological (cameras, pylons, monitors) typical of the metropolitan vision machine.
[12] Mayo was assistant cameraman on Almodóvar's Mujeres al borde de un ataque de nervios (Women on the Verge on a Nervous

Breakdown, 1988) and principal cinematographer on Tacones lejanos (High Heels, 1991). For full details of his career see Francisco Llinás, Directores de fotografía del cine español (Madrid: Filmoteca Española, 1989): 462-463.

[13] The most influential, and most hostile, is Angel Fernández Santos in El País (6 November 1993). The title of his review ("La ley del desastre") recalls the title of his earlier review of La ley del deseo (The Law of Desire, 1987): "La ley del exceso", ironically so, given that one of his chief complaints against Kika is its supposed sterile repetition and self-citation. Once more, French critics vindicate terms taken to be negative by Spaniards, who remain faithful to the ideal of a 'well made script': Strauss (Pedro Almodovar 125) praises the apparent "incoherence" of the plot which he takes to be a freedom from the dictates of narrative convention.

[14] This is the position of a sympathetic British critic such as Jonathan Romney: "Time to Strike Camp", New Statesman and Society (1 July 1994).

[15] The internal citation here is from Husserl, L'Origine de la géométrie.

# III. Feminist Discourses: Reclaiming Subjectivities

# Gender and Difference in *Fin de siglo* Literary Discourse

Susan Kirkpatrick
University of California, San Diego.

I want to begin my presentation today by invoking the angel of the hearth, Restoration Spain's presiding figure of feminine subjectivity. I invoke her because I want to focus on a decade in which her power was on the wane, the decade of the 1890s, in which the Restoration system first showed symptoms of stress under the pressure of social tensions, economic development and world events. In the nineties, throughout Europe and America, the doctrine of separate spheres and the strictly domestic concept of woman's nature was being challenged by a rising bourgeois feminist movement that claimed equality in education and work opportunities, in legal and property rights, and even in political rights. Although there was no organized nineteenth-century feminist movement in Spain, echoes of debates about the "woman question" circulated in the Peninsular press and lecture halls, and the prestigious voice of Emilia Pardo Bazán articulated women's claim to equality in most areas of human endeavor.[1] Nowhere in all her writings in favor of parity for women does doña Emilia put her case more succinctly than in her 1890 introduction to an unmemorable collection of poetry by another woman: "en el reino de las letras no hay, como en las iglesias protestantes, *lado de las mujeres* y *lado de los hombres* ("Dos palabras," x). Through such assertions, Pardo Bazán invigorated the circulation in Spanish culture of the notion that, except perhaps in the area of human reproduction, women were essentially *like* men rather than different from them.

Claims of this sort aroused throughout the cultural field a virulent response affirming sexual difference as the ground of social organization. Positioning himself as a rational arbiter in the debate, *Clarín* offers an authoritative statement of the dominant gender ideology in a late article in which he reads Nietzsche against the feminists. Explaining somewhat mockingly to his Spanish public the German philosoher's anti-feminist and misogynist arguments, *Clarín* attempts to situate himself between the two extremes: "Me apresuro a decir que no se crea, por el tono que vengo empleando, que yo condeno en absoluto las opinions de Nietzsche acerca del feminismo. Me parece que tiene razón en algunas cosas" (Alas, 202). Where Nietzsche is right, according to *Clarín,* is in his insistence on women's "carácter de *sexo opuesto*, de complemento *diferente*" (205; original emphasis). He is willing to grant the feminists that women's educational and legal position should be improved, but "sin reconocerlas la *equivalencia masculina*; viendo en ellas, *naturalmente*, algo, no superior ni inferior al hombre, sino de diferencia complementaria" (206).

Although *Clarín*'s rhetorical strategy in the article on Nietzsche is to affirm the irreducible difference between the sexes as a self-evident axiom of rational discourse, he had revealed his sense that modernity was undermining such certainties in Su único hijo, his last completed novel. Exemplifying the confusion of genders in the passive protagonist and his virago wife, this narrative clearly links the erosion of difference to the breakdown of fundamental systems of social organization and meaning, figured in the collapse of secure paternity in the final scene when the protagonist learns he may not be the father of his newly christened son. As Beth Wietelmann Bauer has observed, "Su único hijo links paternity to promiscuity, both in the narrower, sexual acceptat;ion and in the broader sense of the confusing, mixing, and relaxation of limits and boundaries." This occurs, she points out, in "the principal systems of social exchange, . . . language, money and marriage" (2). Indeed, *Clarín*'s novel expresses the perception, common to a broad spectrum of writing in his time, that the conditions of modernity had led to a collapse of stable categories such as gender--and this anxiety intensified discursive attention to sexual difference.

Another important novel of the 1890s, published in the same year as Su único hijo, deals also with the issue of sexual difference and feminist claims to equivalence. Galdós's Tristana takes up in a less overtly misogynist way a woman's desire to break out of the dependence imposed by the dominant notion of feminine subordination. In the plot devised by Galdós, Tristana's aspirations to freedom and independence are defeated by a form of biological destiny, the illness that in requiring the amputation of her leg, imprisons her within the sphere prescribed for women--in the house and in the kitchen. Yet the heavily ironic tone of Galdós's concluding vignette of don Lope and Tristana as a pious bourgeois couple does not present this image of complementary sexual difference as either natural ordesirable. In this, Galdós's attitude contrasts with the nostalgia for an unquestioned patriarchal order conveyed by *Clarín*'s representation of the promiscuous, topsy-turvy world of Su único hijo. Yet both writers are preoccupied with discourses and practices that threaten to erase the distinction between genders, and ultimately both treat such developments as a synecdoche for changes in social organization as a whole: a social organization which Galdós represents as resistant to change and which *Clarín* sees as susceptible to dissolution.

At the end of the nineteenth century, then, gender difference and gender confusion became key tropes in discourse about society and culture. This was true not only in literary fiction, but also in writing about literature and about the cultural regeneration of the Spanish nation. As we shall see in some examples of this discourse, the rhetorical figuration of femininity split open the reigning ideological image of woman as domestic angel to reveal the negative valuations it covered up. This process is readily apparent in the two novels mentioned already. Emma Valcárcel, the wife of *Clarín*'s protagonist and the mother of his putative son, is described as a vampire and represented as a hysteric with an insatiable sexual appetite. The angel of this novel, dubbed Serafina by the sarcastic author, is the protagonist's vapid mistress, a third-rate singer who longs for bourgeois security. The image of the angel is also made ironic by Galdós, whose narrator calls Tristana a doll with wings. And the text makes it clear that her wings--her aspirations to transcendence--are the symptoms of an unbalanced psyche whose flights of imagination symbolically annihilate the man she loves, for the real Horacio is gradually displaced by an idealized invention of her desire as the addressee of her letters. Similarly denigrating images of femininity--as perverse, pathological, weak-minded, and dangerous--become the operative elements in much of the other *find de siglo* rhetoric deploying the tropes of gender.

The discourse of gender difference was particularly prominent in discussions of the supposed degeneration overtaking Western Europe, discussions that spread obsessively from positivist social science through literary and aesthetic criticism to arguments about national identity. In Spain, as well as in the rest of Europe, an influential source of such discourse was the new discipline of criminology, formed at the intersection of jurisprudence and physical anthropology by the Italian Cesare Lombroso and his followers. Claiming a scientific authority made plausible by the predominance of positivist thought at the time,

Lombroso made Darwin's idea that women were less evolutionarily advanced than men a tenet of his system of distinguishing between normal and delinquent types by physical characteristics. Another of Lombroso's contentions--that the man of genius, the artist, was frequently not only abnormal, but also degenerate--projected his ideas into discussions of literary culture. Max Nordau, declaring himself a disciple of Lombroso, popularized and expanded on this notion in his hugely successful Degeneration (1893), which was translated into Spanish by Nicolás Salmerón.

Salmerón's prologue to the translation will give us a good idea of the form in which the discourse of degeneration circulated in Spain. Nordau, says Salmerón, by moving through "el hospital de histéricos y degenerados en que han convertido a las grandes ciudades" has found the "manifestaciones fundamentales de la perturbación intelectual de nuestros contemporáneos" (ix). These symptoms suggest, according to Salmerón, "la inquietud sombría de un terror de agotamiento, de agonía de una sociedad entera, de todo un periodo de la historia que llega a su fin" (ix). The representation of the end of the century as the end of a social formation was frequently linked by positivists with fears of the physiological exhaustion of the race, a conveniently ambiguous term into which the whole human race, capitalist society, and the people of whichever nation was being talked about were conflated. Salmerón conforms to this pattern in his application of Nordau's ideas to the state of Spanish culture. He argues that the aesthetic symptoms of degeneration catalogued by Nordau are rarely manifested in Spanish literary life, not because it is innately healthy, but rather because of its inherent weakness. "Nuestra vida intelectual civilizada es muy reducida; es un mero reflejo, una imitación, un plagio sin grandez de las corrientes europeas que la moda y el *snobismo* nos impone." Our literary youth are influenced by Ibsen, Tolstoy and Wagner, he says, "pero todo esto permanece en estado pasivo, no se traduce en obras estéticas ni literarias . . ." (xii). With its references to imitativeness and passivity, Salmerón's language subtly feminizes the image he constructs of contemporary Spanish culture: nineteenth-century Spanish criticism had repeated *ad nauseam* just these charges against wome writers. The feminizing trope and its implications become explicit when Salmerón reaches his peroration. He asserts that degenerate aesthetic tendencies have only produced in Spain a vauge hybrid mixture, whose effect has been "la nota femenina, ficticia, hipócrita, sin energías," "una literatura que no hiere, sino araña, no pinta, sino esboza, no tiene alientos varoniles, sino suspiros, no sabe rugir embravecida, se agita con impotente coraje" (xiv). In making clear that degeneration is a form of feminization, Salmerón expresses a fundamental feature of the discourse he is using. It is significant, I think, that Salmerón finds in the feminization of contemporary Spanish culture rather than in its excessive refinement or sophistication the symptoms that match those described by Nordau for the rest of Europe.

The threat to civilization--and, more immediately, to the Spanish nation--posed by the end of the century in this view is a collapse of the distinction between the sexes caused by men becoming more like women. Salmerón's figurative language describing Nordau suggests what he regards as the remedy to Spanish culture's degeneration into femininity: "¿Vuelve acaso el rostro el cirujano cuando se encuentra con la gangrena?" he asks, claiming that Nordau "trata de atajar las corrupciones sociales . . . , mostrando en toda su desnudez lo hondo del mal, lo inminente delconagio, procurando combatirle con decisión y energía" (xv). The gendered terms of the remedy are clear: the intrepid, energetic male surgeon must cut out the spreading contagion of the feminine if Spain is to regain cultural health and vitality.

The discourse linking femininity with the pathological and the degenerate, and hence connecting national decadence with feminization, appeared also in Literaturas malsanas, an 1894 work so closely resembling Degeneration in some of its arguments that its author, the Catalan anarquist Pompeyo Gener, was accused of plagiarism.[2] The anxiety to maintain gender difference through abjection of the feminine is palpable in Gener's insistent distinction between decadent and "unhealthy" art, to be condemned in all its forms, and art that is vital or "virile"--terms he uses interchangeably. Gener's book, interestingly enough, was attacked with scathing humor by none other than *Clarín*, who also lost no opportunity to ridicule as flagrant pseudoscience the claims of Nordau and the Lombroso school. The irony here is that while Alas rejected the claims of these writers to scientificity, he subscribes to the figurative logic of their rhetoric insofar as it concerned gender and nation. Consider the following passage from a piece in which *Clarín* mentions with scorn the "pseudoscience" "que está haciendo estragos, particularmente en Italia" (Almas, xviii): it pains him, he says, that young Latin American writers "tome[n] casi siempre el camino que va al peor abismo, al aniquilamiento de la savia española, de la enjundia castiza . . . . ¿Cómo no he de censurar a esa literatura americana que no asimila lo extraño, sino que se disuelve en lo extraño; que, con una especie de éxtasis, muy mal empleado, se pierde en el *objeto amado*, pasa a el, y viene a convertirse en un triste remedo de los tiquis miquis de las letras francesas . . . . ?" (Almas xii). *Clarín*'s figurative feminization of the Latin-American writer--in this context a synonym of "modernista"--by attributing to him imitativeness, promiscuity and passive loss of identity is most fully understood as a response to the situation in which he wrote the piece. These words belong to the prologue that Alas contributed with openly confessed reluctance to a book published in Paris and written by the Guatemalan journalist Enrique Gómez Carrillo. Titled Almas y cerebros: Historias sentimentales, intimidades parisienses, this book is indeed promiscuous, beginning with a satire of the Lombroso/Nordau thesis concerning the pathology of the modern artist, continuing with journalistic interviews juxtaposing Nordau himself with such decadent or sexually ambiguous figures as J-K. Huysmans and Oscar Wilde, and concluding with a long summary of recent studies by Krafft-Ebing and others on sexual perversion. *Clarín*'s attempt to shore up an uncontaminated core of Spanish masculinity is thus enmeshed in what it resists: the promiscuous modern discourse that threatens to dissolve the boundaries protecting national and gendered identities. It is symptomatic of the insinuating ower of the new discourses that *Clarín* found himself seduced or inveigled into providing the prologue for a book so obviously distasteful to him.

The year of publication of Gómez Carrillo's book and *Clarín*'s introduction is also charged with significance. Almas y cerebros appeared in 1898. In the aftermath of the Spanish defeat, the rhetoric linking the feminine with degeneration, pathology and promiscuous "aniquilación de la enjundia castiza" would intensify. Literary critics and historians would construct a narrative that carefully distinguished the virile, energetic, *castizo* Generation of 1898 from the degenerate, feminized and non-national *modernistas*.[3] And the compensatory image of Salmerón's iron surgeon would exercise its force in Spanish culture decades beyond its appearance in the regenerationist exhortations of Joaquín Costa. But on the other hand--and here I conclude by opening a new chapter--this same rhetoric undermined the sway of the *ángel del hogar* as the predominant and normative image of woman. This figure's decorously oppressive hold on Spanish women began to weaken, and more militant feminist voices emerged to contest the abject images of femininity produced by patriarchal anxiety at the turn of the century.

Notes

[1] A useful index of feminist organizing activity in the 1890s is found in the national councils that formed under the auspices of the International Council of Women: between 1888 and 1900, national councils were founded in Canada, Germany, England, Sweden, Italy, Holland, Denmark and Switzerland, but not in Spain (see Fraisee, 493).
[2] Maristany concludes that Gener had not read *Degeneration* when he wrote *Literaturas malsanas*, but was influenced by the same intellectual currents (25-26).
[3] This has been argued by Cardwell, and Blasco Pascual also mentions the gender factor's role in the distinction between *modernismo* and *noventayochistas*.

## Works Cited

Alas, Leopoldo *Clarín*. "Nietzsche y las mujeres." Obra olvidada. Ed. Antonio Ramos Gascón. Madrid: Ed, Júcar, 1973. 198-209. Originally published in El Español, 6-7 September, 1899.

- - - . Prólogo. Almas y cerebros. Por Enrique Gómez Carrillo. Paris: Garnier, 1898. vii-xxii.

Bauer, Beth Wietelmann. "Something Lost: Translation, Transaction, and Travesty in Clarín's Su único hijo." Paper read at the Midwest Modern Languages Association meeting in Minneapolis, November, 1993.

Blasco Pascual, Javier. "De 'oráculos' y de 'cenicientas': La crítica ante el fin de siglo español." ¿Qué es el modernismo? Nueva encuesta, nuevas lecturas. Ed. Richard A. Cardwell and Bernard McGuirk. Boulder, CO: Society for Spanish and Spanish-American Studies, 1993. 59-86.

Fraisse, Geneviève and Michele Perrot, eds. A History of Women: Emerging Feminism from Revolution to World War. Cambridge, MA and London: Harvard University Pr., 1993. Vol. 4.

Gener, Pompeyo. Literaturas malsanas. Madrid: Fernando Fe, 1894.

Maristany del Rayo, Lluis. El artista y sus congéneres. Resumen de la Tesis. Barcelona: Universitat de Barcelona, 1985.

Pardo Bazán, Emilia. "Dos palabras." Prologue to Poesías by Carolina Valencia. Palencia: Alonso y Martínez, 1890. vii-xi.

Salmerón y García, Nicolás. Prólogo. Degeneración by Max Nordau. Trans. Nicolás Salmerón. Madrid: Fernando Fe, 1902. v-xvi.

Scanlon, Geraldine M. La polémica feminista en la España contemporánea, 1868-1974. 2nd ed. Madrid: Akal, 1986.

# The Question of the Political Subject in Nineteenth-Century Spanish Domestic Discourse

Cristina Enríquez de Salamanca
Yale University.

Scholars working on nineteenth-century Spanish culture have proposed two conflicting models for female subjectivity produced by this bourgeois society: the model of "difference" and the model of "equality."

The first model, "difference," emerges in the work of Bridget Aldaraca, Alicia Andreu, Alda Blanco, Lou Charnon-Deutsch, Catherine Jagoe, and Susan Kirkpatrick, among others; they have shown how a domestic ideal of womanhood became visible in Spanish culture supported by medical, social, and religious discourses, how it acquired increasing momentum through the first half of the nineteenth-century, and how a Rousseaunian image of woman, el "ángel del hogar," was consolidated by 1850. This representation of the female subject appeared in sharp contrast to its male counterpart. Women, domestic ideology said, did not have the qualities required by liberal thinking to participate in the social contract. They were not "rational beings," as men were. Thus, only men were by nature political beings

Historical research has also shown the production of another ideal of womanhood grounded in the model of equality, an ideal which most would characterize as "feminist." Susan Kirpatrick has found a rebellious and proto-feminist consciousness in the Spanish tradition of women's writing originating in the 1840's, a consciousness that, Kirpatrick says, disappeared in the literature of mass consumption after 1850, but whose legacy was preserved in the feminist or contestatory voices of the female producers of high culture of late nineteenth-century Spain (Las Románticas 292, 295). Jiménez Morell also sees feminist thinking in the mid-century utopian socialism of the female Fouerist press. For Geraldine M. Scanlon, a feminist impulse was derived from the revision of old values brought about by the 1868 Revolution, and in particular, from the Krausistas's support of women's educational and legal rights (La polémica feminista 7-8). In contrast to the model of "difference," the equality model claimed that rationality was not a male privilege but an attribute owned by all, and that therefore, women should enjoy legal and political rights equal to those of men.

Logically then, we might see the 1932 Republican Constitution's granting female suffrage, as a result of the equality model, the result of a consciousness raised by the actions of political parties and social groups concerned with advancing political, legal and economic rights for women. A close look at the history of Spanish women's suffrage, however, reveals that the link between women's inclusion into the formal political order and movements supporting the model of equality was extremely weak.

First, the history of the Spanish feminist movement shows its late and fragile development. Most feminist scholars characterize the Spanish feminist movement with negative traits -- slow, weak, and ineffective -- and they also see its birth taking place within the second decade of the twentieth century, that is, a few years before the 1932 Republican Constitution. Second, nineteenth and early twentieth century Parliamentary debates on women's suffrage proposed the right to vote for those women exercising *patria potestas* or legal power over their children. That is, it was precisely in their maternal function that women were thought of as political subjects. Third, by looking at the position taken on women's suffrage by progressive and conservative sectors during the years preceding the Second Republic, one cannot possibly conclude that the efforts to place women within the formal political order were linked to movements supporting the model of equality. As the research of Concha Fagoaga shows, during this time "progressive" parties -- who theoretically most supported women's equal legal and political rights -- either ignored or plainly opposed women's suffrage, and on the contrary, women's political rights were, in one way or another, promoted particularly by those social forces and political parties which backed up the doctrine of separate spheres for men and women.

A reading of Spanish history thus reveals that paradoxically this bourgeois society demanded political rights for the domestic woman, and that this happened in spite of liberal theory's argument that women were naturally estranged from the rules of citizenship. In other words, whereas Enlightened thinking said that woman's nature consists precisely in being "Nature," as the opposite of "Reason," and that the domestic sphere was the locus of the irrational, Spanish bourgeois culture detected in the epitome of the maternal model, the domestic angel, a kind of rationality which made her inclusion in the political system logically unavoidable. This could have happened only if it had become previously possible to imagine a political subjectivity for women within the public sphere, and if gender ideology had been re-articulated in such a way that the irrational and disorderly features attributed to the female subject and her private sphere could come to be perceived in a different light. I will show that this change in perception took place primarily through the agency of nineteenth-century serial novels, manual conduct books, and didactic works written by female domestic writers from 1850 to 1880.

Mid-nineteenth century conservative governments established through printing laws a series of controls on writing aimed at protecting the domestic family. One such control was a literary program enunciated by powerful politician Cándido Nocedal, and no doubt disseminated by judicial structures, since Nocedal held such positions as Secretary of the Cabinet and *Fiscal de Imprenta*. Through his law of July 13, 1857, and through the speech he delivered to the Royal Academy of the Spanish Language, Nocedal articulated a poetics of domesticity in which the written language of the domestic woman was defined as a literary language and a rational form. In the above mentioned speech Nocedal said, "Let your eyes return to your childhood,"

> let's evoke the memories of your early years . . . and you will find arguments in favor of the novel. Do you remember those stories that a tender and adorable mother told you? . . . Those children's stories, no doubt, were a sort of novel. Didn't you see in villages an old lady telling awesome local traditions by the fire . . .Those traditions are novels . . . neither that old lady nor your mothers would ever intend to pervert and hurt your heart Especially mothers! What statesman will ever surpass in foresight a mother when her child and his education are in question?
>
> [volved los ojos, Señores, a vuestra infancia; evocad los recuerdos de vuestros primeros años . . . y hallaréis argumentos en favor de la novela. ¿Os acordáis de aquellos cuentos que una tierna y adorada madre os narraba? . . . Pues aquellos cuentos, no hay que dudarlo, eran una especie de novelas. No vísteis

> en las aldeas una anciana refiriendo junto al hogar portentosas tradiciones de la comarca . . . Pues esas tradiciones son novelas . . . ni aquella anciana, ni vuestras madres, se habían de proponer, pervirtiéndole y dañándole, endulzar vuestro corazón. ¡Las madres sobre todo! ¿Qué hombre de estado vencerá nunca en previsión a una madre cuando de sus hijos se trata y en su educación se ocupa?]
>
> ("Discurso del Excmo. Señor Don Cándido Nocedal" 380-381)

What we encounter in Nocedal's words is that the language of the domestic woman acquires normativity. The voice of the angel of the house is defined as literature, and literature implies literary expertise, that is knowledge of aesthetics and rational thought. The articulation of this poetics was no doubt an act of male control on women's intellectual activities, but it paradoxically empowered women, even though it neither applied only to them nor did it expand the topics on which they were authorized to write.

In consonance with Nocedal's program, from 1850 to 1880 many female writers promoted a domestic ideal of womanhood best known as "el ángel del hogar." However, in their writings these authors represented a wealth of female characters who were, at the same time, angels of the house and professional or amateur writers. Fusing their own subjectivity as writers with that of the domestic woman represented in their works, and with their potential female readers, domestic writers established a link between author, fictional characters, and readers, so that the image of a Virtuous Domestic Woman who was also a writing subject circulated within the public sphere of letters, moving from "real" people (the domestic writers) to fictional characters and to readers. Given the enthusiastic audience response -- a fact that cannot be disputed if we look at the many reprints of those works during the nineteenth-century -- there is good reason to argue that the image of a Virtuous Domestic Woman who was also a writing subject became a fantasy shared by the members of a female community.

Domestic writing thus provided female authors with the technical means for "representing" a kind of imagined community, conjuring up in their reader's minds an imagined world of women who were all simultaneously doing the same things. This -- a precise analog of the idea of the nation theorized by Benedict Anderson in Imagined Communities (24-25) -- made possible the birth of a communal identity of authors and readers within the public sphere on the basis of their gender. Bourgeois domestic culture characterized as "feminine" such topics as the concerns of everyday life, dress, manners, decoration, and the emotions of family relationships. Through essays and articles, periodicals and books dealing with these topics, and also through legal instruments such as Nocedal's program, a sphere of letters infused with sexual difference was built by the community of domestic writers and readers. A "domestic sisterhood" was born, that is, a network of women continuing the "lyrical sisterhood" that Kirpatrick has shown us was established by romantic writers (Las Románticas 79-87), but engaged in literary and didactic writings whose common ground was domesticity.

The "domestic sisterhood" however, shared an ideal -- the Virtuous Woman/ Writing subject -- who was not unruly "Nature." On the contrary, while absolutely private and devoted to domestic life, this ideal female subject was also simultaneously a writing subject; she was "culta," or cultivated, which is to say, in nineteenth-century terms she was individuated. In this way, the female realm conceptually associated with the reproduction and maintenance of the body was occupied by a female subject in whom an extremely powerful link between two notions of the female was forged: "woman" and the female writing subject.

Mid-century domestic writing also revised what Spanish society considered "natural" to women by transforming the home into a realm of the beautiful, the elegant, a realm of taste and art. Domestic writing said that there was beauty in daily life that could only be produced and experienced by "el angel del hogar." This aesthetics -- best represented in the writings of Pilar Sinués -- valued a number of activities that the masculine tradition of philosophical aesthetics would never have considered art: dress, decoration, manners. Through the image of the Virtuous Woman that united authors, exemplary characters, and readers, nineteenth-century women readers were called upon to contribute a content to the "real" domestic space they inhabited: that content was "beauty." Due to the aesthetic quality the domestic woman brought to everyday life, the practical affairs of everyday life became non "natural" in the traditional sense. Through the aesthetics of private life, the natural processes of birth, death, and other physical processes were transformed into cultural signs of affection, vigilance and duty. In this way, if the moral order embodied by the domestic woman was not the same as the moral order of the political sphere, neither was it the same as the primitive order of "savage" life.

The irrational and disorderly features attributed to the female subject came also to be perceived in a different light when domestic writing transferred the custody of children from male to female. Through a process similar to that outlined for North-American culture by Mary Ryan, Spanish female domestic writers seized upon the affections as the foundation of child-rearing, and attributed to the mother the basic functions of child care, emotional support and social reproduction. The role given to women as moral educators conferred on them the power of making their children into "good citizens," children whose personalities could be fit to lead an adult life. The mother thus came to take charge of ordering what Terry Eagleton calls the 'aesthetic' realm of "habits, pieties, sentiments and affections" (The Ideology of Aesthetics 23), so that society's norms would become internalized, producing a self-limitation of behavior which would make the controlling and repressive mechanisms of society superfluous. The final goal of this process was investing children with inner power, control and restrain, that is, with rationality.

Yet, one cannot communicate what one lacks. Therefore, the role given to the domestic angel had to rely on the implicit acknowledgment of her rationality, even if her rationality -- understood as the ability to socialize the human spirit -- was associated with emotional processes and not with the realm of pure thought considered proper to the male subject, and thus "his" rationality. It is in this light that one has to understand the 1889 Civil Code granting to the mother *patria potestas* or legal power over her children. Through this right, the mother was allowed to govern the actions of her under-aged children within the confines of the domestic sphere and to perform in some cases juridical acts in their name in the outside world. Legal discourse thus admitted the mother's capacity for discernment, that is, that the mother had the rationality her offspring lacked.

The transfer or expansion of children's custody from male to female just described provided a necessary stage in the process of widening women's sphere. What could have initially been just a "private" practice of "private" individuals, went beyond the boundaries of family life, since it was precisely in their maternal functions that women were proposed as political subjects in 1877, 1878, 1907, and 1908 Parliamentary debates on women's suffrage. This meant that a link between the rationalities of the private and the public spheres had been perceived and granted institutional space by Spanish culture.

When read against the background of political theory and practice in nineteenth-century Spain, this reformulation of the domestic by women writers was an act of momentous political importance. Through the reciprocal actions of legal and political discourses, on the one hand, and a domestic writing, on the other, women could be seen as political subjects, according to Liberal theory. and in particular, according to its specific Spanish nineteenth-century version known in political history as doctrinaire liberalism.

Although restricting women's intellectual production, Spanish nineteenth century culture nevertheless legitimized domestic writing, and defined a way in which a woman could write. Once this right had been granted, society could not avoid recognizing its corollary: women's ownership of intellectual property. To modern culture, intellectual property is not a "thing" one acquires only through a contract, as one does in the case of material goods, land or capital. Intellectual property is not an exterior good that comes to the hands of a person, but rather, in a sense, is part of the human being; it is an objectification of something that originates inside the mind. Whether or not a woman in bourgeois liberal society held property in her own body, and whether or not she could be the owner of such common properties as "material goods, lands and capital," the fact is that she could become an intellectual property owner.

This modifies the rationale that excludes women from the social contract. This rationale argues that women do not hold their own bodies as property, and that therefore, they can not claim self ownership. However, if a woman owns intellectual property, it can be argued to some degree that she also owns at least a part of her own "person." As a consequence of this capacity, women could be seen as subjects who were both owners of their own goods and owners of their own "persons." This position, partially converted women into "individuals," (in the Liberal sense) who enjoyed rationality, who were "endowed with the attributes and capacities necessary to enter into contracts."

Moreover, as intellectual property owners, women could be seen as individuals according to the Spanish nineteenth-century political system, known as doctrinaire liberalism. In other words, women could be also characterized as "literatos." They could form part of one of the categories that nineteenth-century Spanish Constitutional Laws defined as political subjects, or *capacidades*, that is, as one of those subjects identified through their rationality as capable of governing themselves and therefore capable of governing others. Article one of the Electoral Law of June 26, 1890, defined as electors "all male Spaniards, twenty five years of age or older." This was the first time that the legislature explicitly excluded female suffrage introducing the term "male" as one of the traits electors had to enjoy. Even in a negative form, the legislature was implicitly acknowledging that, potentially, women could become electors. This acknowledgment, I believe, was at least partially due to the agency of nineteenth-century female domestic writing from 1850 to 1880.

In this study I have participated in a debate that has taken place since the eighteenth-century in most Western countries. The central issue of such debate is whether or not, and in what exact terms, can women be considered political subjects equal to men. Likewise Liberal theoreticians, many past and contemporary feminists find incompatible the model of equality and the model of difference, arguing that the second model only deterred women from citizenship. I have on the contrary proposed a paradox: that the model of "difference" eventually made the ground for women's citizenship. Through the image of a Virtuous Domestic Woman who was also a writing subject, nineteenth-century female domestic writers made possible the birth of a female imagined community within the public sphere, thus bringing middle-class women into social and political visibility. By doing so and also by revising what Spanish society considered "natural" to women, the domestic writing produced by women during the second half of the nineteenth-century in Spain became a major factor in constructing not only the basis for, but also the consciousness of, a political identity which achieved political recognition only in 1932, when the Republican Constitution granted female suffrage.

## Works Cited

Aldaraca, Bridget. "El ángel del hogar:' the Cult of Domesticity in Nineteenth-Century Spain." Theory and Practice of Feminist Literary Criticism. Gabriela Mora and Karen S. Van Hooft (Eds.) Ypsilanti, Mich.: Bilingual Press, 1982. 62-87.

---. "The Medical Construction of the Feminine Subject." Cultural and Historical Grounding for Hispanic and Luso-Brazilian Feminist Literary Criticism. Hernán Vidal (Ed.) Minneapolis: Institute for the Study of Ideologies and Literature, 1989. 395-413.

---. El 'ángel del hogar:' Galdós y la ideología de la domesticidad en España. Trans. Vivian Ramos. Madrid: Visor, 1992. El 'ángel del hogar:' Galdós and the Ideology of Domesticity in Spain. Chapel Hill: North Carolina Studies in the Romance Languages and Literatures, 1991.

Anderson, Benedict. Imagined Communities. Reflections on the Origin and Spread of Nationalism. London: Verso Edition and NLB, 1983.

Andreu, Alicia G. Ed. & Introd. "La cruz del Olivar por Faustina Sáez de Melgar: Un modelo literario en la vida de Isidora Rufete." Anales Galdosianos 1980; 14 (supp.): 1-68. Introd., 7-16.

---. Galdós y la literatura popular. Madrid: Sociedad General Española de Librería, 1982.

---. "Arte y consumo. Ángela Grassi y El Correo de la Moda." Nuevo Hispanismo 1 (Winter 1982): 123-35.

Blanco, Alda. "Domesticity, Education and the Woman Writer: Spain 1850-1880." Cultural and Historical Grounding for Hispanic and Luso-Brazilian Feminist Literary Criticism. Hernán Vidal (Ed.) Minneapolis: Institute for the Study of Ideologies and Literature, 1989. 373-94.

---. "The Moral Imperative for Women Writers." Indiana Journal of Hispanic Literatures. 2. 1 (Fall 1993): 91-110.

---. "Gender and National Identity: The Novel in Nineteenth-Century Spanish Literary History." Civilization and its Others. Eds., Mary Layoun and Jane Tylus. (forthcoming).

---. "Pilar Sinués de Marco." Encyclopedia of Continental Women Writers. Katharine Wilson (Ed.) New York: Garland Press, 1991. 157-58.

Charnon-Deutsch, Lou. "On Desire and Domesticity in Nineteenth-Century Women's Novels." Revista Canadiense de Estudios Hispánicos. XIV. 3 (Spring 1990): 395-414.

---. "The Social Masochism of the Nineteenth-Century Domestic Novel." Indiana Journal of Hispanic Literatures. 2.1. (Fall 1993): 111-31.

---. Narratives of Desire. Nineteenth-Century Spanish Fiction by Women. University Park, Pennsylvania: The Pennsylvania State University Press, 1994.

Eagleton, Terry. The Ideology of the Aesthetics. Oxford: Basil Blackwell, 1990.

Fagoaga, Concha. La voz y el voto de las mujeres españolas. El sufragismo en España 1877-1931. Barcelona: Icaria, 1985.

Jagoe, Catherine. Ambiguous Angels: Gender in the Novels of Galdós. Berkeley/Los Angeles/London: University of California Press, 1994.

---. "María del Pilar Sinués de Marco (1835-1893)." Spanish Women Writers: A Bio-Bibliographical Sourcebook. Linda G. Levine, Ellen E. Marson, and Gloria F. Waldman (Eds.) Westport, Connecticut, London: Greenwood Press, 1993. 473-84.

---. "Noncanonical Novels and the Question of Quality." Revista de Estudios Hispánicos 27.3 (1993): 427-36.

Jiménez Morell, Inmaculada. La prensa femenina en España (desde sus orígenes a 1868). Madrid: Ediciones de la Torre, 1992.

Kirpatrick, Susan. Las Románticas. Women Writers and Subjectivity in Spain 1835-1850. Berkeley/Los Angeles/London: University of California Press, 1989.

Nocedal, Cándido. "Discurso del Excmo Señor Don Cándido Nocedal." Discursos leídos en las recepciones públicas que ha celebrado desde 1847 La Real Academia Española. Vol 2. Madrid: Imprenta Nacional, 1860. 371-82.

Scanlon, Geraldine. La polémica feminista en la España contemporánea (1868-1974). Madrid: Siglo XXI, 1976. 2nd ed. Madrid: Ediciones Akal, 1986.

# The Construction of Subjectivity in Contemporary Women Writers of Catalonia

Geraldine Cleary Nichols
University of Florida

Nancy Miller has lamented that the death of the author was solemnly declared by Western intellectuals just as women began edging not toward authorship--they had written for centuries--but toward the authority of canonicity. "The postmodern decision that the author is dead, and subjective agency along with him, does not necessarily work for women" she notes (qtd. in de Lauretis 106). Declaring the demise of the author is a way of "reading women out" before they have had a chance to be read or read in. "When a theory of the text . . . chooses the spider's web over the spider, and the concept of textuality called the 'writerly' chooses the threads of lace over the lacemaker . . . , the productive agency of the subject is self-consciously erased" and "the question of identity itself" is foreclosed ("Arachnologies" 271). If the writer's identity is elided, gender becomes immaterial, and there are "no bodies that matter" (to use Judith Butler's cogent title). Miller summarizes: "tearer and torn trade places in a linguistic play of indifference" ("Arachnologies" 283). This notion rebarbatively echoes New Criticism, with its valorization of the well-wrought and perfectly deracinated urn, the literary artifact so masterful that all mankind could thrill to its purportedly universal sentiments.

Miller rejects this attempt to efface the writing subject, arguing that we know too little about the subjectivity of women writers--or the materiality of their lives--to foreclose further investigation in the name of a "(new) monolith of anonymous textuality" (qtd. in de Lauretis 104). She urges critics to continue probing the differential conditions affecting the production of women's literature, to theorize the ways in which gender and other social and discursive constructs are embodied in writing. "When we tear the web of women's texts we may discover in the representations of writing itself the marks of the grossly material, the sometimes brutal traces of the culture of gender; the inscriptions of its political structures" ("Arachnologies" 275).

Such is precisely my intention today: to suggest some of the conditions, both material and discursive, which have shaped the complex subjectivity of three contemporary Catalan writers--

Ana María Moix, Montserrat Roig, and Carme Riera--and to look briefly at one aspect of their fiction for traces, inscriptions and marks of their configuration as writing subjects.

The three were born into the comfortable homes of the Catalan bourgeoisie between 1946 and 1948: ground zero for some of the fiercest ideological wars ever waged on the Iberian peninsula, which is no sloucher in this category. If the subject is constructed through ideology, as Althusser posits, our writers, weaned on ideologies as inflexible as they were contradictory and stifling for women, had every prospect of growing up schizophrenic. As Catholics, they were brought up as daughters of Eve--and of Mary--in the theocratic state resulting from the unification of Francoism and National-Catholicism. As daughters of an ultra-orthodox bourgeoisie in some of the darkest moments of its troubled history--the years between the collapse of the Second Republic and the death of the Catalans' bête noir, Franco--they would have been schooled to be perfect, and perfectly useless, ladies.[1] Given the precariousness of the Catalan bourgeois class under Franco, the daughters' training would have been intensified by their female affines as a way to strengthen the internal cohesion of the group.

Not simply bourgeois Catholics, the young women were also Catalans, and as they matured the voice Catalan nationalism, with its nineteenth-century gender schemata, grew ever louder. Just as the discourse of feminism began to be heard, these young writers were exposed to the ideas of Catalan nationalism, which urged them to imitate Teresa, la Ben Plantada of Eugeni d'Ors. Teresa, a woman who "owes herself to the [Catalan] Race," ["es deu a la Raça" (86)], is praiseworthy for many reasons, including the fact that she is like a faithful mule. There is, D'Ors wrote, "the same profound, tranquil, noble obedience in both" ["La mateixa profunda, tranquil.la, noble obediència en tots dos" (qtd. in Capmany, 62)]. Marxism too competed for the allegiance of young people of their generation. Moix, for example, read El capital when she was 13, "and I would have let them burn me at the stake for my Marxist dogmatism," she wrote to Chacel ["A los trece (entre 12 y 13) leí El Capital, y me hubiese dejado quemar viva por mi dogmatismo marxista." (Cartas 159)]. Marxism provided yet another dissonance in the discursive cacophony that surrounded them, insofar as it condemned the class distinctions that their families had inculcated in them so carefully, divisions that had structured their domestic and urban space from the time they were born.

If, to use another formulation, "it is in language that people constitute themselves as subjects" (Belsey 47), our young writers had it no easier, for they were reared in the midst of virulent but eerily muted language wars, with Catalan the language of the family and Castilian that of the servants, the state, the school and church. In any case, women are "particularly contradictory subjects," as Belsey writes, because they "participate both in the liberal humanist discourse of freedom, self-determination and rationality and at the same time in the specifically feminine discourse offered by society of submission, relative inadequacy and irrational intuition" (qtd. in Hutcheon 82).

The concept of identity as a matrix or combination of subject positions is particularly useful in analyzing writers like Moix, Roig, and Riera, interpellated from their earliest years by multiple and often conflicting messages about what it meant to be a proper young lady; a Catholic; a Catalan in a Castilian state; a woman; a Catalan woman; unlike one's brothers; unlike one's servants; and sexual (less was more in this discourse). "The female subject is a site of differences," De Lauretis writes: "differences that are not only sexual or only racial, economic, or (sub)cultural, but all of these together, and often enough at odds with each other" (14).

Riera, Roig, and Moix write, then, from what we might call a composite--or even fractured--subjectivity. Insofar as they write about the discursively constructed world which scripted their silence, they step outside that world, and are insider/outsiders; insofar as they write against the grain, from or about the selvage rather than the cloth itself, they create another discourse, one which may in time encourage new forms of subjectivity, and create, in Toni Morrison's words, "something else to be" (qtd. in De Lauretis 10).

Several metaphors come to mind to illustrate the subjectivity of the person who is partly inside and partly outside, in what Rachel du Plessis calls an "(ambiguously) nonhegemonic" position (15). Sarah Schuyler uses a term which she found in Christina Stead and Zora Neale Hurston, "cracked plate," to denote a person who projects a unified identity but is actually crisscrossed with fault lines or contradictions. Mercè Rodoreda provides us with another. This brilliant novelist, who spent half her life in exile from Franco's Spain, and whose subjectivity had more cracks than plate, took Stendhal's novelistic mirror, perfect for reflecting a humanist vision of a unified world, and changed it to fit her own reality. She put this mirror in the hands of a servant suddenly crowned mistress in a world turned upside down by the civil war, and had her fall down the stairs. I quote from the novel, Mirall trencat (1983) [the Broken Mirror], in my own translation: "The mirror broke. The pieces stayed in the frame except for a few that fell out. She picked them up and stuck them in the spaces where they seemed to fit. These bits of mirror, all uneven: did they reflect things as they were?" ["El mirall s'havia trencat. Els bocins s'aguantaven en el marc, però uns quants havien saltat a fora. Els anava agafant i els anava encabint en els buits on li semblava que encaixaven. Les miques de mirall, desnivellades, reflectien les coses tal com eren?" (258-59)].

Montserrat Roig provides another image for the oxymoronic identity of the insider/outsider, taken from the quintessentially Catalan, quintessentially female world of textiles. It is the term selvage, that is, "the edge of a woven fabric finished so as to prevent raveling, often in a narrow tape effect, different from the body of the fabric" (Random House). In L'òpera quotidiana an older woman, part of the Catalan bourgeoisie but impoverished, eccentric, and estranged from her family, uses the word--voraviu in Catalan--to explain how she has survived her marginalization by valuing that which is--like herself--unrepresented in hegemonic discourse. She explains her strategy of survival to another outsider, the young xarnega--non-Catalan immigrant--whom she employs: "Life isn't worth it unless we can be transported by perfect beauty, because it has no words and it enters you directly, it goes right into the selvage of your senses, do you know what selvage means, dear? well, it's an edge or border so strong it can't be unraveled, and that is what you feel when the music penetrates you so profoundly, that nothing can unravel you" ["La vida no val la pena sinó és per a emocionar-nos amb la bellesa absoluta, perquè no té paraules i t'entra directament dins del voraviu dels sentits, saps què és el voraviu, nena?, doncs una vora que, de tant resistent, no es pot desfilar, i així és allò que sents quan la música t'entra ben endintre, que res no se't pot desfilar . . . ." (83-84)].

Cracked plates, broken mirrors, resistant, resonant selvages; such are our writers' subjectivities. But how do these fragile, intricate identities get projected, without splintering, into literature, and how are they reflected in the form and content of that literature? "A model that sees hegemony articulated among multiple determinations obviously poses serious representational problems," R. Radhakrishnan observes about historiographical discourse in postcolonial India. "If the categories of gender, sexuality, nationality, or class can neither speak for the totality nor for one another but are yet implicated in one another relationally, how is the historical subject to produce a narrative from such a radical relationality, a relationality without recourse?" (81).

Radical relationality or "absent totality" (Radhakrishnan 81), what Sarah Schuyler describes as "riding the margin, the borderline, the slash mark, the crack in the plate of gendered subjectivity" (85), is in fact a salient characteristic of the fiction of Moix, Riera, and Roig. Several areas of their writing--narrative voice and structuring, characterization, subject matter, and themes--problematize the inside/outside distinction, underlining the ways in which different discursive formations brand different people outcasts, denying them any possibility of recourse or change. They mobilize these novelistic elements and others to explore the relationship of the part to the whole and the particular to the universal, as well as the links between the silenced and the spoken, the proscribed and the preferred. Their fiction gives voice, accords a place in public discourse to the part, the particular, the excluded and the heretofore muted.

Time constraints will only permit me to look at one of these narrative elements in the fiction of Moix, Riera and Roig. I have chosen narrative voice, since it is the area most clearly related, as we shall see, to their discursive formation as writing subjects. Young women who aspire to write must simultaneously block out the culture's siren calls to passivity and silence while at the same time listening actively for scraps of voices at other frequencies, voices that might speak to them if only they could hear them over the static and the cultural jamming.

Beginning in their adolescence, the three writers began to search for models, for literary voices that they could plausibly imitate. Adrienne Rich has written of the "peculiar confusion" felt by "the girl or woman who tries to write because she is peculiarly susceptible to language. She goes to poetry or fiction looking for <u>her</u> way of being in the world, since she too has been putting words and images together; she is looking eagerly for guides, maps, possibilities; and over and over . . . she comes up against something that negates everything she is about: she meets the image of Woman in books written by men. She finds a terror and a dream, she finds a beautiful pale face, she finds La Belle Dame Sans Merci . . . but precisely what she does not find is that absorbed, drudging, puzzled, sometimes inspired creature, herself, who sits at a desk trying to put words together" (qtd. in Miller, "Changing" 109).

Ana Moix was 18 when she read Rosa Chacel's Teresa, a book she and Pere Ginferrer had found in the backroom of a bookstore, where the owner kept books proscribed by government censors (Nichols 104). She immediately initiated correspondence with the exiled writer, whom she begged to answer her questions about "the construction of the novel, and how one should write today, and why (a question that perplexes and bothers me)" ["Me encantaría . . . que tolerara mis preguntas sobre la construcción de la novela, cómo se debe escribir hoy, y por qué (cosa que me preocupa e inquieta)" (Cartas 150)]. She extols Ana María Matute's writing to Chacel, confessing: "I began to write reading her work, when I was 12, and since then I have followed her work with an interest verging on fervor" ["yo empecé a escribir leyendo su obra, a los 12 años, y desde entonces he seguido su obra con un interés hecho casi fervor" (Cartas 152)]. When she met Matute, she writes in another letter, it "was something like the profanation of her art. Now everything I desire exists, and if it is possible, it is real. This imprinted me, literarily and as a human being" ["Conocerla era algo así como la profanación de su arte. Ahora todo lo que quiero existe, y si es posible es real. Me marcó literariamente y humanamente" (Cartas 159)].

Montserrat Roig carried out a similar search for literary models and roots, an exploration she limited to authors writing in Catalan: "Literarily, I have always searched within strictly circumscribed parameters . . . ; I was from a very Catalan family, and I began reading in Catalan when I was four . . . . From adolescence on, I always identified my language and not Castilian with literature" ["literariamente yo he buceado siempre en unas preocupaciones muy estrictas . . . ; he pertenecido a una familia muy catalana en donde desde los cuatro años he leído en catalán . . . . Puedo decir que a partir de la adolescencia siempre identificaba mi lengua y no la castellana con la literatura" (Nichols 147)]. She read voraciously: "In those years I had my idols and my anti-idols; I had a love-hate relationship with my language and my literature. That's what I lived for, not for anything else" ["Entonces tenía mis maestros y mis anti-maestros; tenía una relación dialéctica de amor y odio con mi propia lengua y mi propia literatura. Yo me nutría de eso, no vivía de otras cosas" (Nichols 148)]. Like Moix, Roig's search for a predecessor whose work would speak to her, authorize and inspire her to continue the daily battle with the blank page, ended when she found a voice that could be hers, a woman's voice: "For me, the great revelation, the person who brought me to literature ... was Mercè Rodoreda. The day I read La Plaça del Diamant, just published, it made a huge impression on me . . . . And if she impressed me so much, it's not because she was better or worse than Virginia Woolf, for example, but because she said to me that it was possible to write in my language" ["Para mí la gran revelación, la persona que me acercó a la literature sin saberlo ella--o creo que nunca lo supo--fue Mercè Rodoreda. Yo el día que leí La Plaça del Diamant, recién publicada, me hizo una impresión tremenda . . . . Y si ella me impresionó tanto, no es porque ella fuese mejor o peor que Virginia Woolf, por ejemplo, sino porque ella me estaba diciendo que en mi propia lengua era posible escribir" (Nichols 148-49)].

Carme Riera's account of her search for plausible models is similar: "I looked for predecessors, because it was very difficult for me to write without knowing what roots I had, in the sense of a language elaborated by women. For a woman, writing is in a sense a double rebellion. First, because she's writing; she is a woman, and for that reason she's marginalized. Second, because she is writing in a language that also marginalizes her; the language itself leaves women out" ["Yo busqué antecedentes, porque me era muy difícil escribir sin saber qué raíces había tenido yo atrás, en el sentido de una lengua trabajada por mujeres, ¿no? Para una mujer, escribir literatura es en cierto modo una rebeldía doble. Primero, porque está escribiendo; es mujer y por esto está marginada. Y segundo, es el hecho de que está escribiendo en una lengua que también la margina, la propia lengua margina a las mujeres"(Nichols 203)].

Once the aspiring writers had found a few voices in their own register, voices which had defied the general mandate for women to bite their tongue, or "fer muts i a la gàbia" [shut up and get in the cage] as the Catalan expression has it, other problems surfaced. How could they, their heads filled with contradictory messages in two languages, imbue a solitary narrative voice with sufficient objectivity and authority to tell a single story? And in what language? They knew from their own experience that there is no single story, unentangled with others; that for them, at least, there was no inexpugnable prospect--what Buero Vallejo in El tragaluz, echoing Ortega y Gasset, has called the "perspectiva de Dios"--from which they could emit thunderous dictates. For them, there was no fiercely protected space from which to paint quinces.[2] They would be obliged to find another way, other places, from which to write about another, piecemeal, reality.

It must have become clear to these nascent writers that, in order to reflect with fidelity any part of the world they knew, they would have to signal the partiality of their vision. And that is why so much of their fiction is couched in first or second person, in a voice--sometimes written, sometimes spoken--that calls attention to itself as limited, dubitative, and idiosyncratic. In Moix, for example, we have Julia, of the eponymous novel; Ismael, in Walter, ¿por qué te fuiste?; the narrator of the stories "Dedicatoria," "Redacción," "Yo soy tu extraña historia" and "Las virtudes peligrosas." In Riera: "Te deix, amor, la mar com a penyora," "Jo pos per testimoni les gavines," and most of the other stories in the eponymous collections; in Epitelis tendríssims, all but two of the stories, and seven of nineteen in Contra l'amor en companyia. Of Riera's novels, Qüestió d'amor propi--as an epistolary novel--is all first person; Una primavera per a Domenico Guarini is predominantly second and then first person, and half of Joc de Miralls is told from the narrator's first-person point of view. Roig's fiction is also full of narrators in first person, often more than one to a novel, as in Ramona, adéu and L'hora violeta. L'òpera quotidiana, as its title suggests, is structured like an opera, with singing parts for all major participants. In La veu melodiosa the narration seems to be third person but turns out, in the end, to have been controlled by a narrator so unsure of herself that she remains effectively hidden until the epilogue.

Through such manipulation of narrative voice, the three authors repeatedly call attention to language as constructor, deformer, and filter of reality. Riera assiduously marks her characters' speech, foregrounding its peculiarities. Her early stories take the form of skaz[3] delivered by Mallorcan country women; in Una primavera per a Domenico Guarini, she foregrounds the diverse registers of Catalan, Mallorcan, and Valencian; several stories of Contra l'amor en companyia, revolve around the uses and abuses of bureaucratese, or the clichéd language of gossip columnists; in her latest work, Dins el darrer blau, seventeenth-century Mallorcan alternates with contemporaneous hagiographic Castilian.

Moix's fiction also calls attention to speech, to speakers, and to discourse as configurers of the real. In "Antes del almuerzo" and "Erase una vez," the only reality is that which has been fixed in the always already written text or the invariant story formulas; no one can advance beyond those beginnings. In "Las nutrias no piensan en el futuro," a child's family rejects him because his speech, unlike that of the father's parrot, is not an exact echo of the parents'. Moix's "Redacción" criticizes hypocrisy, a practice which consists of saying one thing and doing another. As an aside, let me note that all three writers excoriate hypocrisy in their fiction; perhaps because their "peculiar susceptibility" to language and their perception of discourse as structurer of reality made them especially sensitive to this eminently bourgeois vice. At any rate, "Redacción" takes the form of a boy's composition for religion class; the assigned topic is "God and the creation of the world." He writes in the composition that he realizes it will be given a failing grade, precisely because he has followed the teacher's directions. "Exponed, libremente, problemas, dudas y soluciones personales." These are patently hypocritical words, saying one thing when the opposite is true, for in Francoist schools "thinking freely about religious issues" was a discursive impossibility.

Finally, Moix and Riera and Roig make abundant use of irony in their fiction. This is a double-voicing that calls attention to the spoken--as untrue--and thus to the unspoken, to that which is left out of representation. In a letter to Chacel, Moix explains how she has double voiced a story--I believe she is talking about "Dedicatoria"--and why she felt impelled to do so: to ensure a faithful representation of that which mainstream stories and history omit, which is the reality Moix and other orphans of discourse like her have lived:

> I invent my story, on top of one that I wrote some time ago and on top of the current one; at the same time, I cry about it, which lends it the air of a second story--or perhaps it is the primary one. I think that History hides an infinite number of (hi)stories behind its capital H, which is why it is written with a capital and not a little letter.

> HISTORY is the most restricted and least plausible of stories, and for that reason it has to be studied and learned. The other (hi)story emerges from the imagination enmeshed in time; it emerges from those of us who find ourselves on the other side from those who tell our stories and attempt to explain what we are. . . .
>
> [Invento mi historia, sobre la que creé hace tiempo y sobre la que es; al mismo tiempo lloro sobre ella, esto le pone un tono de segunda historia --tal vez sea la primera--. Pienso que la Historia oculta infinidades de historias tras su hache mayúscula, y en esto está la razón de que se escriba con hache grande y no pequeña.
>
> La HISTORIA es la más pequeña, la más inverosímil, por eso hay que estudiarla y aprenderla. La otra es patrimonio de la imaginación en el tiempo, de nosotros en la otra cara de los otros que nos cuentan e intentan explicar . . . (Cartas 172).

Beyond their use of narrative voice and structuring, the three writers also employ characterization to deconstruct a world divided neatly between insiders and outsiders, favorite sons and black sheep; to point toward Toni Morrison's "something else to be." In Dins el darrer blau, Riera rescues the historic figure Rafel Valls from ignominy, showing her fictional Gabriel Valls to have been the most honorable of men. Roig recreates voices and characters lost because they were not considered important; Moix has us observe the quite plausible and affecting ruminations of the almost mad. There are schizophrenic, mirrored, doubled, fragmented and otherwise unstably bounded characters throughout their fiction, as well as liars, writers, seducers, visionaries, dogmatists and fools. History, religion, romantic love, maternal devotion and patriotism are shown to be fiction, discourses with ulterior motives, with aims on the unsuspecting.

By way of conclusion, I would like to read a poem Ana Moix, age 19, wrote and sent to Rosa Chacel. Even at that age, Moix knew that she was not--could never be--represented in any of the competing discourses that sought to construct her comme il faut.

we would have to begin again
to learn the abc's all over
for everything, learn to say everything
learn how to learn to forget
what we forgot when we learned
to forget. We must invent
our vocabulary. There are
words, words, words. There are
words that no one has spoken, I know
we have felt but never read them
never spoken, never written, never
thought; felt them, but
never in letters, in signs, in notes
it is imperative to begin again
we have to learn to not read
without reading, we have learn again how
to write without writing silence.

tendríamos que volver a empezar
aprender de nuevo el abecé
de todo, aprender a decir todo
aprender a aprender el olvido
de lo que olvidamos al aprender
a olvidar. Hemos de inventar
nuestro vocabulario. Hay
palabras, palabras, palabras. Hay
palabras que nadie ha dicho, lo sé,
las hemos sentido, nunca leído,
nunca dicho, nunca escrito, nunca
pensado; sentido sí, pero
nunca en letras, ni signos, ni notas,
es necesario volver a empezar
hemos de aprender a no leer
sin leer, hemos de volver a saber
escribir sin escribir el silencio.

Whether we consider them broken but reassembled mirrors, cracked plates, or selvages, what we find in these three authors is a single unwavering conviction: that the voice which sounds from the margin merits a place in discourse. The competing ideologies they heard as girls and young women--the "words, words, words" of Moix's poem--only coincided in prescribing secondary, silenced status to the women they would become. That message, summarized in one of Riera's early stories as "girls don't ask questions; they behave like good little girls" ["ses nines no fan preguntes, ses nines són bones al.lotes" (Jo pos per testimoni les gavines 41)] is precisely the one they would flout most systematically. Because these three writers learned, indeed, to write without inscribing silence.

Notes

[1] The adolescent Ana Moix wrote to Rosa Chacel in 1965: "I repeat that the the environment which has surrounded me--externally--is the Catalonian. I think that the bourgeoisie in Catalonia is the most bourgeois in the world" ["insisto en que el medio que me ha rodeado--por fuera--ha sido catalán. Creo que los burgueses catalanes son los más burgueses que existen" (Cartas 158)].

[2] Víctor Erice's film, El sol del membrillo,"was shown as part of the "Spain Today" conference. The film depicts Spanish artist Antonio López's months-long contemplation and painting of a quince tree. Everyone in the household accommodates and defers to his need to concentrate on the quince. His wife, for example, runs the household and serves as his business manager. When she tries one evening to finish a long-abandoned portrait of López, her attempt is given short shrift not simply in the film, but in reality as well: López falls asleep after a few minutes of modeling.

[3] Skaz is a Russian word used by Mikhail Bakhtin in Problems of Dostoevsky's Poetics. The translator's note defines it as: "a technique or mode of narration that imitates the oral speech of an individualized narrator" (8, note b). Carme Arnau uses the term "escriptura parlada" (spoken writing) to describe the same technique in Rodoreda (see Arnau 118-21).

## Works Cited

Arnau, Carme. Introducció a la narrativa de Mercè Rodoreda: el mite de la infantesa. Barcelona: Edicions 62, 1979.

Bakhtin, Mikhail. Problems of Dostoevsky's Poetics. Ed. and trans. Caryl Emerson. Minneapolis: U of Minnesota P, 1984.

Belsey, Catherine. "Constructing the subject: deconstructing the text." Feminist Criticism and Social Change: Sex, Class and Race in Literature and Culture. Eds. Judith Newton and Deborah Rosenfelt. New York: Methuen, 1985. 45-64.

Campany, Maria Aurèlia. La Dona Catalana. Barcelona: Mateu, 1968.

Cartas a Rosa Chacel. Ed. Ana Rodríguez Fischer. Madrid: Cátedra, 1992.

D'Ors, Eugeni. La Ben Plantada/Gualba, la de mil veus. 1911/1915. Rpt. Barcelona: Edicions 62, 1980.

De Lauretis, Teresa. "Feminist Studies/Critical Studies: Issues, Terms, and Contexts." De Lauretis 1-19.

---. ed. Feminist Studies/Critical Studies. Bloomington: Indiana UP, 1986.

duPlessis, Rachel Blau. The Pink Guitar: Writing as Feminist Practice. New York: Routledge, 1990.

Hutcheon, Linda. "Subject in/of/to History and His Story." Diacritics 16 (1986): 78-91.

Miller, Nancy K. "Arachnologies: The Woman, the Text, and the Critic." The Poetics of Gender. Ed. Nancy K. Miller. New York: Columbia UP, 1986. 270-95.

---. "Changing the Subject: Authorship, Writing, and the Reader." De Lauretis 102-20.

Moix, Ana María. Ese chico pelirrojo a quien veo cada día. Barcelona: Lumen, 1971.

Nichols, Geraldine C. Escribir, espacio propio: Laforet, Matute, Moix, Tusquets, Riera y Roig por sí mismas. Minneapolis: Institute for the Study of Ideologies and Literature, 1989.

Radhakrishnan, R. "Nationalism, Gender, and the Narrative of Identity." Nationalisms and Sexualities. Eds. Andrew Parker, Mary Russo, Doris Sommer, and Patricia Yaeger. New York: Routledge, 1992. 77-95.

Random House Dictionary of the English Language. 2nd ed.

Riera, Carme. Jo pos per testimoni les gavines. Barcelona: Laia, 1977.

Rodoreda, Mercè. Mirall trencat. Barcelona: Edicions 62 i "la Caixa," 1983.

Roig, Montserrat. Digues que m'estimes encara que sigui mentida. Sobre el plaer solitari d'escriure i el vici compartit de llegir. Barcelona, Edicions 62, 1991.

---. L'òpera quotidiana. Barcelona: Planeta, 1982.

Schuyler, Sarah. "Double-Dealing Fictions." Genders 9 (1990): 75-92.

# IV. Looking Ahead in Iberian Studies

# 2001 poesía española: ¿la frontera final?

Dionisio Cañas
Baruch College, CUNY

Uno no se puede imaginar un mundo peor y mejor que el nuestro: en él conviven el terror y el humanismo, la alegría y el miedo cotidianos, el subdesarrollo más extremo y el progreso tecnológico más alucinante, las enfermadades sin solución y las operaciones hechas a través de un ordenador, la artesanía y el arte creado por computadoras, la total incomunicación interpersonal y las superautopistas para la comunicación internacional, el hecho de que no conocemos ni a nuestros propios vecinos y a la vez nos llegan en directo las imágenes de una guerra desde un país remoto, el hambre mundial y los miles de planes para adelgazar, disfrutamos de más libertades civiles que nunca y, sin embargo, tenemos más rejas en nuestras ventanas, más cerrojos en nuestras puertas, más condones en nuestros dormitorios, y mientras unos niños hablan de viajes interplanetarios en Nueva York, otros se mueren de hambre en Haití... etc, etc, etc. ¿Y los poetas qué? ¿Sobre qué escriben los poetas? ¿A quién se dirigen los poetas? ¿Hacia dónde va el pensamiento, la poesía, y el libro como vehículo principal de la escritura?

## El pensamiento y la poesía ante el siglo XXI

El camino del pensamiento y de la poesía ha sido largo, confuso y caótico a veces, pero sin duda estamos asistiendo a una nueva forma de ver el mundo y de vernos a nosotros mismos. "El futuro posee una nueva superación independiente del espíritu auténticamente filosófico y metafísico", escribía Max Scheler al final de su obra Conocimiento y trabajo (1926). De esto hace ya casi setenta años, y hoy sólo se puede decir que las varias tendencias del pensamiento posmoderno han intentado, con mayor o menor acierto, abrir un nuevo espacio filosófico y estético para que, al margen de la filosofía, aquella anunciada superación pueda tener lugar.

Mas el pensamiento existencial venía ya, desde antes de la guerra civil española, haciéndose el portavoz de un pesimismo que en absoluto era nuevo, y que con los horrores de las dos guerras mundiales se convertirá en un cáncer que haría imposible cualquier hedonismo entusiasta. Las interpretaciones existencialistas de la filosofía y del mundo nos llevaron por tortuosas avenidas, las cuales, por un lado, nos hicieron creer que la única salvación estaba en la conciencia de que nadie podía salvarnos; y esto a pesar de algunos pensadores de la existencia, cristianos, que eran más optimistas. Por otro lado, una línea de la fenomenología iniciada por Husserl, y también las vanguardias artísticas, aunque sin ignorar el fundamental pesimismo que ha caracterizado gran parte del siglo XX, subrayarían el poder creador e imaginativo del ser humano, el cual lo religaba con sus orígenes y lo proyectaba hacia el futuro como un poder resistente a cualquier caos. Me parece que es precisamente esta mezcla de descreencia existencial de una parte, y entusiasmo creador, por la otra, la que de algún modo está dando forma al sujeto posmoderno en general (y al poético en particular), es decir, al sujeto del siglo XXI.

Pero en lo fundamental, desde el mismo siglo XIX, la técnica y la idea de progreso científico han sido vistas por los pensadores y los poetas occidentales como la verdadera amenaza frente a la hegemonía de cualquier pensamiento filosófico o poético. Las religiones de todo orden se han apoderado de las mentes más blandas, y hemos llegado a la paradójica situación, de que junto a un vertiginoso progreso tecnológico y científico, conviven hoy en día en Occidente un auténtico primitivismo de orden mágico-religioso. Esta aparente anomalía es un buen abono para que la imaginación ocupe de nuevo un lugar preponderante en nuestra sociedad, y para facilitar al poeta, en su sentido más primitivo y colectivo, la posibilidad de que pueda volver a ser oído.

Por lo tanto, donde los pensadores que analizan nuestro fin de siglo perciben sólo signos alarmantes de caos, dispersión, debilidad, apocalipsis, nosotros vemos la agitada base de aquella superación de la que hablaba Max Scheler. Y estamos así convencidos de que la alianza entre tecnología e imaginación, individuo y sociedad, originalidad y colectivismo, ocupará un lugar central en la materialización de dicha superación; aunque los soportes, los medios y los géneros de la literatura, y del arte, se verán necesariamente alterados y enriquecidos.

**La poesía española: actualidad y futuro**

La poesía española posmoderna ha sido marcada por varias antologías, algunos libros de crítica, y algún que otro debate. Enumero varios de esos esfuerzos: la Teoría de la expresión poética (1952) de Carlos Bousoño; el debate entre poesía como conocimiento y poesía como comunicación, que tuvo lugar en la década de los 50; dos libros de ensayos de José Olivio Jiménez, Cinco poetas del tiempo (1964) y Diez años de poesía española (1972); la antología Nueve novísimos (1970) de José María Castellet; y el impacto de la obra de Luis Cernuda, y de casi todos los poetas de los años 50, en la poesía que se ha venido haciendo hasta hoy día. Es posible que no todo el mundo esté de acuerdo con lo que acabo de señalar, pero es evidente que, para bien o para mal, en la lista que he ofrecido aparecen referentes de los cuales no puede prescindir nadie (ya sea para defenderlos o atacarlos) que quiera acercarse a la poesía española publicada después de 1939.

Hace unos meses José María Parreño (poeta y gestor cultural) señalaba "la lluvia de críticas que está recibiendo la poesía de la experiencia --convertida en tendencia dominante en la última generación de poetas". Y es que en 1992 aparecieron ya dos prólogos que aparentemente querían marcar otra dirección para la poesía española de este fin de siglo: la introducción a una selección de la poesía de Leopoldo María Panero realizada por Jenaro Talens, y el texto "Language: un proyecto radical para la escritura de fin de siglo" de Esteban Pujals Gesalí, el cual sirve de introducción a su libro La lengua radical. Antología de la poesía norteamericana contemporánea. En ambos casos se ataca la tradición cernudiana vigente en la poesía española de la segunda mitad de este siglo, la preponderancia de una idea de la poesía cuyo referente principal es el autor, la actitud acrítica frente al lenguaje de la poesía actual, y los mecanismos de canonización de la poesía: desde las universidades hasta los cenáculos poéticos como son los premios, las revistas literarias y las editoriales especializadas en este género. Por lo contrario, estos dos críticos nos proponen una poesía que es mucho más radical, que critica la literatura "como práctica social y como 'imagen' institucional".

A través de los poetas norteamericanos antologados por Pujals Gesalí, éste nos propone una escritura que se convierta "en una actividad a un tiempo utópica y comprometida al máximo con su tiempo y lugar". Y Talens nos dice que la obra de Leopoldo María Panero representa "una de las escrituras más lúcidas y radicales que ha producido la poesía española de esta segunda mitad de siglo". No sé si serán estos los dos modelos que darán un nuevo vigor a la poesía española del siglo XXI, pero sin duda pueden ser un horizonte para que nuestra poesía se aparte parcialmente del continuismo que la ha caracterizado hasta ahora.

No obstante, hay que tener presente que un movimiento de los años cuarenta, el Postismo, ya había hecho de la imaginación su arma principal, del lenguaje en sí y del subconsciente sus fuentes de inspiración, y en muchos casos querían que sus obras coincidieran con "la producción artística de los perturbados mentales".

En lo que se refiere a la poesía española producida en las dos últimas décadas, se podría señalar que casi todos los poetas tienen una vocación de poetas menores, que casi todos escriben bien, muy bien, como aplicados alumnos de un instituto de la poesía, que muchos son muy buenos chicos y chicas, que todos publican libros, demasiados libros... Por lo tanto, nadie se puede quejar; por lo tanto, nadie puede decir que la poesía no goza de una buena salud en España; aunque yo sí quiero decir que estamos viviendo el momento del siglo XX cargado de menos ambición estética en poesía por parte de los mismos creadores, y de una carencia absoluta de pasión y de intensidad.

Esta poesía última no nos propone casi nada nuevo: se alimenta de una nostalgia temporalista y de un ensimismamiento narcisista y, en su mayoría (no toda), continúa la línea de Luis Cernuda (cuya admirable obra no es culpable de que sus imitadores sean tan insípidos), y de los poetas de la generación del 50, que tanto ha dependido de la experiencia personal, resorte y móvil casi exclusivos de sus obras. Me refiero, claro está, a la poesía escrita por los poetas españoles que oscilan entre los veinte y los cincuenta años; que vendrían a ser los "maestros" en la poesía del año 2.001. Existen algunas excepciones como el antes mencionado Leopoldo María Panero, Antón Reixa (poeta, roquero, video-artista y realizador de performances), Rogelio López Cuenca (poeta, artista, y miembro de uno de los colectivos más importantes de España, "Parejo School"), entre otros esfuerzos como los de la "Compañía Poética Momentánea", algunos libros escritos por mujeres, figuras aisladas como Roger Wolfe y algunos más que yo desconozco.

Pero es grande la resistencia a cambios significativos en la poesía española actual. En un tomito cuyo título es ¿Por qué no es útil la literatura?, Luis García Montero (poeta) y Antonio Muñoz Molina (narrador) se erigen en fervientes defensores del libro como objeto indispensable para que la dignidad del ser humano siga mejorando, y también se hacen los abanderados de una cultura para gente "normal". Este último concepto de una supuesta "normalidad" no lo acabo de entender, pero lo que sí me queda claro es que estos dos autores se pronuncian por la defensa del libro como único medio para conservar los valores "eternos" de la sociedad occidental. Se suman así, estos dos escritores, a los alarmados intelectuales que ven en los medios audiovisuales una amenaza apocaplíptica para la cultura de Occidente.

Es esta una forma de reacción negativa que se inició en el arte y la literatura con la aparición de la fotografía y el cine, la radio y los discos, y después con la televisión. Ahora nos encontramos desbordados por una avalancha de nuevos medios y de nuevas tecnologías, y frente a éstas más de un escritor español siente que su oficio está llamado a desaparecer. Esta preocupación, con ser respetable, no deja de parecernos un error fundamental, porque primero se asume que las personas "normales" son tan estúpidas que se dejan comer la conciencia por los nuevos medios y que, ellos, los escritores son los únicos seres elogiables por sus altas ocupaciones y preocupaciones librescas.

Donde debería existir una "colaboración", una alianza entre los nuevos, y ya incluso viejos medios audiovisules, y la poesía, nuestros poetas se empeñan en ofrecer una resistencia despreciativa que en absoluto beneficia a las futuras generaciones de poetas españoles. Ya hemos llegado tarde y precipitadamente a la modernidad, y ahora nos queremos encerrar en un conservadurismo que hará más notable nuestro característico retraso cultural. No se trata de que yo recomiende el que sea necesario lanzarse ciegamente al uso indiscriminado de las nuevas tecnologías, sino que me parece una irresponsabilidad hablar de una manera tan obtusa, en lugar de tomar una postura tolerante, abierta, con miras al futuro. Asustar al lector medio con la amenaza de que la apertura cultural posmoderna es una nueva forma de la barbarie, de la desculturación, del embrutecimiento, creo que parte de un conservadurismo que en absoluto facilita la entrada de nuestra poesía en el siglo XXI.

Pedro Provencio, en una serie de artículos publicados en la revista Cuadernos Hispanoamericanos (el último es del mes de septiembre de 1994), habla de que vivimos en la poesía española de las dos últimas décadas "una época de auténtica contrarreforma estética", es decir, en una época antivanguardista. Como los tres escritores antes mencionados, Provencio critica, o más bien describe educadamente, los estragos que está haciendo la poesía de la experiencia en España. No obstante, aquél señala que dentro de las filas de nuestra poesía actual se encuentran algunos poetas que "podrían en cualquier momento ofrecernos la sorpresa de una obra arriesgada y ambiciosa", y ofrece varios nombres que parecen ser, según él, la tabla de salvación para nuestra poesía, estos son: Jorge Riechmann, Luisa Castro, Blanca Andreu, Juan Carlos Suñén y José María Parreño. Y finalmente, concluye Provencio que "se trataría del posible final de la poesía española tal como se entiende a sí misma. Y quizás ése es el síntoma mayor de agotamiento: que nuestra poesía, en sus principales manifestaciones como estamento rígido, tiende a evitar todo riesgo de ver mermada su autoidentificación".

Dentro de la poesía española de esta mitad de siglo se encuentran a veces poemas, y otras veces libros enteros --como Don de la ebriedad, de Claudio Rodríguez o Libro de las alucinaciones de José Hierro--, que sin duda están llamados a sobrevivir (entre los cuales alguno del mismo Luis García Montero) frente a cualquier cambio de los gustos y de la orientación de la poesía española que se avecina. Ni la radicalidad de ciertas propuestas, ni el continuismo de gran parte de nuestra poesía son la frontera final de la producción poética española, sino que quien sepa apropiarse de los elementos poéticos diversos de nuestra poesía y que, ya sea colectiva o idividualmente, pueda adaptarlos, renovándolos, a la época histórica y al momento cultural que le toque vivir en el siglo XXI, será nuestro poeta futuro.

## ¿La frontera final? Entre el libro y los medios audiovisuales

Pronto se cumplirán los cien años de la publicación de un libro fundamental para el género de la novela de ciencia ficción, pero también imprescidible para entender nuestra cultura actual: me refiero a La máquina del tiempo de G.H.Wells. En la película que se hizo basada en esta novela, hay un momento dado donde el personaje central, en un remotísimo siglo del futuro, constata que los pocos libros que existen están todos ya carcomidos por el tiempo y se deshacen sólo con tocarlos, y ese personaje reacciona con estupor y con ira contra aquella supuesta civilización del futuro. Posteriormente, cuando el protagonista vuelve a su presente, finales del siglo XIX, decide que prefiere retornar a aquel futuro del que había regresado, y el enigma final es que se lleva con él tres libros, de los cuales no sabemos el autor ni los títulos.

A partir de la obra de Wells la ciencia ficción va a tratar frecuentemente el tema del libro; ya sea insertando alguna discusión lateral respecto al libro o haciendolo a éste el eje de la ficción. Este es el caso de Fahrenheit 451, la novela de Ray Bradbury, donde la quema de libros es el objeto y la ocupación principal del gobierno. Y en 1984 de George Orwell, donde leer y memorizar libros es igualmente un "pecado social".

Si le hiciéramos caso a las novelas y las películas de ciencia ficción constataríamos con cierto terror, para algunos, que en el futuro habrá pocos libros, que estos libros serán como una rareza decorativa (como en el caso de la película Blade Runner y de la serie de televisión Star Trek), que entre estos libros habrá algunos clásicos solamente, que estos libros serán leídos en escasas ocasiones, como si fuera un lujo. Nuestros millones de libros parece que irán a parar a un banco de información de infinita pequeñez y, posiblemente, gran parte de la poesía española del siglo XX desaparecerá en el limbo de la informática. A menos que los poetas comprendan que el progreso, en poesía como en las demás artes, significa "el empleo del material en el sucesivo estadio más avanzado de la dialéctica histórica" (Theodor W. Adorno); o sea, la escritura, el lenguaje, en su contexto social dinámico y moviéndose a la vez que ese mismo contexto.

Para los que nos hemos educado entre libros y materiales impresos, la posible desaparición de estos como forma central de la cultura, nos parecerá una aberración difícil de entender. Pero para las personas que se eduquen en el siglo XXI, por lo menos en el mundo occidental, y si no sucede ninguna catástrofe, el libro convivirá con medios electrónicos de comunicación cultural, los cuales han empezado ya ha ser producidos con una celeridad tal que, a los neófitos, nos sorprende y nos desconcierta. Desde las enciclopedias y libros de todo tipo en CD-ROM, los libros electrónicos, la literatura interactiva, hasta el vídeo y la televisión, se está fomentando la cultura a través de unos medios que son ajenos a casi todos los poetas españoles que han empezado a escribir en los últimos veinte años. Maria Victoria Atencia, una poeta de los años 50, acaba de sorprenderme enviando a los críticos su obra completa en disco para ordenador;

supongo que no quiere quedarse rezagada frente a los avances tecnológicos que se anuncian para el siglo XXI.

Pero no hay por qué alarmarse; siempre habrá algún nostálgico de la palabra impresa sobre papel que querrá comprar algún viejo libro del siglo XX. Lo que me parece absurdo es que la mayoría de los críticos y creadores vean el presente y el futuro como un caos, un desorden, una dispersión; aunque, paradójica y contrariamente, en España se tenga la impresión de que estamos viviendo un nuevo Siglo de Oro. Nos falta un aparato crítico y estético que nos pueda servir para analizar objetivamente lo que está ocurriendo en la cultura actual; por esta razón creo que sería mejor limitarse a describir los acontecimientos artísticos, para que esa descripción sea la base de más seguras evaluaciones en el futuro.

La voz de alarma suena frecuentemente entre nuestros intelectuales.... Cuando se quiere descartar o disminuir el valor de algunas obras se habla de "posmodernidad", como una forma de burla contra ciertas manifestaciones que parecen "raras" en la cultura española de hoy. La estupidez y la ceguera intelectual con que se usa este concepto en España, y la frivolidad autoritaria con la que se usa este mismo término entre los nuevos hispanistas en los EE.UU., nos darían para horas de discusión. En otros países es frecuente la misma actitud, pero lo que resulta, a mi entender, menos pertinente es el empeño de algunos intelectuales por deslegitimar gran parte de la cultura actual contrastándola con los cánones de la de otros siglos pasados; digamos que con los valores fijos, seguros, de la bolsa de la cultura. O pretender, con actitud pesimista, que estamos viviendo la crisis de la modernidad; lo cual es una actitud frecuente en escritores que precisamente son producto de las vanguardias (como es el caso de Octavio Paz) y a quienes no les conviene en absoluto que la hegemonía total de la modernidad pierda su vigencia.

El asunto del canon de la literatura occidental ha sido recientemente discutido por Harold Bloom en su libro The Western Canon. Esta obra, que es más bien una autobiografía intelectual del autor, tiene el encanto de que terminamos por ver a través de ella una radiografía clara de la mente de este crítico. Pero si le hacemos caso a sus caprichos se concluiría que la literatura española contemporánea tiene muy pocas posibilidades de formar parte del canon occidental. De todas formas, en las películas de ciencia ficción nunca he visto que se conserve ningún libro de ningún crítico de literatura. Pero no nos preocupemos: al desaparecer los libros de Bloom, y por lo tanto esta charla de hoy, es posible que algún poeta español se salve.

Para terminar me gustaría añadir que probablemente la nueva frontera de la poesía española se encuentre en una revaloración de la imaginación poética, usada ésta como herramienta para expresar y enriquecer nuestra experiencia personal del mundo y de la vida cotidiana. Para esto habrá que recuperar las voces de Vicente Aleixandre, la del Lorca de Poeta en Nueva York, la del Alberti de Sobre los ángeles, la de la poesía de Juan Larrea, y algunos nombres de la posguerra como los antes citados, y a los que añadiría las obras de, Joan Brossa, Carlos Edmundo de Ory, Juan Eduardo Cirlot y Antonio Gamoneda (esto, claro está, limitándome a la poesía peninsular). De igual modo creo que esta revaloración de los elementos más irracionales de la poesía se servirá de todos los medios puestos a la disposición de los nuevos escritores, y no exclusivamente del libro. Igualmente pienso que sin duda la misma realidad existencial y cultural que les toque vivir, a estos poetas del siglo XXI, les ofrecerá un mundo de imágenes nuevas que revitalizarán la empobrecida y debilitada poesía española actual.

Obras Citadas

Adorno, Theodor W. Reacción y progreso y otros ensayos musicales. traducción de José Casanovas. Barcelona: Tusquets, 1970.

Bloom, Harold. The Western Canon. The Books and School of the Ages. New York: Harcourt Brace & Company, 1994.

García Montero, Luis y Antonio Muñoz Molina. ¿Por qué no es útil la literatura? Madrid: Hiperión, 1993.

Parreño, José María. "De la exposición universal del 92 a la indisposición particular del 94." Claves 43, junio de 1994.

Provencio, Pedro. "La últimas tendencias de la lírica española." Cuadernos Hispanoamericanos 531, septiembre de 1994.

Pujals Gesalí. Esteban. Introducción "Language: un proyecto radical para la escritura de fin de siglo." La lengua radical. Antología de la poesía norteamericana contemporánea. Madrid: Gramma, 1992.

Scheler, Max. Conocimiento y trabajo. Buenos Aires: Editorial Nova, Traducción de Nelly Fortuny [1926] 1969.

Talens, Jenaro. "De poesía y su(b)versión. (Reflexiones desde la escritura denotada 'Leopoldo María Panero.'" prólogo a Agujero llamado Nevermore (Selección poética, 1968-1992). Madrid: Cátedra, 1992.

## The Evolution of the Spanish Literary System

Darío Villanueva
Universidade of Santiago de Compostela

This essay represents a sort of continuation of the ninth volume of the Historia y Crítica de la Literatura Española, published in 1992. Francisco Rico had assigned me the task of discussing the Spanish literary history from the death of Franco and the end of his dictatorship in 1975 to the first years of our current decade. I decided at that time, given the almost unsolvable nature of the project, to adopt an innovative methodological perspective, one which I feel very closely identified with as a professor of literary theory. I intended to abandon the idealized concept of the literary as a purely aesthetic field, in favor of analyzing it in terms of a system of social actions, from a totally pragmatic and empirical perspective, as has been done in Germany by the school known as the "Empirische Literaturwissenschaft", led by Siegfried J. Schmit, and in Israel by the Itamar Even-Zohar group with its "Polysystems Theory".

The second stimulus functions as a catalyst for the following pages and is related to the adjective "Spanish" which accompanies the syntagm "literary system" in the title of this essay. Its meaning here is not geopolitical, but linguistic. It does not refer to the literary system which exists in the Spanish state, the constitutional entity made up of sixteen autonomous communities, some of which, like Galicia where I come from, have their own languages which coexist within their territories with the ancient Castilian tongue. On the contrary, it refers to the international system which is built on foundations of a Spanish language reinvented and rewritten in the Americas, where it is spoken and nurtured by literally hundreds of millions of Spanish speaking people.

Even though it is impossible to imagine a literature without a language, the mere presence of a language does not make for sufficient conditions for literature to exist; more so, if the language in itself is already a social phenomenon, which individual speakers can influence within margins that only its great writers have been able to expand significantly. In addition, literature has become today a part of a complex system that includes the creator of the text and his or her readers, but also involves other elements which play a crucial role in deciding whether or not books reach their intended audience and is affected by such institutions as literary criticism and academia Each factor, process or agent of this literary system interacts with and is dependent upon all of the rest, and only from this perspective of looking at these factors as a whole, can the significance of literature be comprehensively understood.

Octavio Paz highlighted these issues in his speech at the Universidad de Alcalá given upon receiving the Cervantes Prize in 1981, when he affirmed that he did not understand literature as simply a collection of authors and books, but as "a society of works" in which the reader's role of co-creator is fundamental. But no less important is the presence of a consolidated literary tradition with its spectrum of themes, procedures and styles, with its canon of universally accepted authorities, of a criticism and didactic structure attentive to its analysis and interpretation, and a cultural industry that through publishing houses, magazines, literary supplements and other related enterprises provide the channels and support for pure creation, and for satisfying the readers' demands. Literature does not come to its end at that mysterious moment of the solitary birth of a poem, a novel, an essay or a play, for really at that moment the text barely has a life of its own away from that of its creator, whose talent, aesthetic perception of reality, vision and personal demons, are reflected in his or her work. In a certain sense, it is at this moment that the text comes into existence and is opened up to a vast panorama with no spatial or chronological limitations.

This notion, that all books an authors are actually contemporaries, and to a certain extent compatriots, is easily assimilated into the old maxim that the homeland of the writer is language. For Jorge Luis Borges, language is our tradition, and every writer is given the chance to change it only slightly; an idea which would also have pleased T.S. Eliot, as he believed, contrary to the romantics, that the originality of a writer shines more brilliantly to the extent that he or she is able to incarnate the tradition from whence they came. Of course, this is not the only way to understand the literature written in a given language, but when this language is as widespread and productive as Spanish is, it constitutes in itself a universe of inexhaustible resources and possibilities, for writers as well as for readers.

In the third Argentinean Congress of Hispanists, which took place in the city of Buenos Aires in May of 1992, several papers were presented evaluating the role of the "Miguel de

Cervantes Prize for literature in Spanish Language" created in 1976, as a new institution especially significant in the contemporary trajectory of a literary "field" or "system" that embraces both continents. That literature in Spanish language was from very early on a communication factor which integrated the peoples on both sides of the Atlantic, is an indisputable fact, and it still is, along with Spanish language, the most solid connection of heritage that unites us, transcending the progression of history, beyond the demands made by our separate nationalities. As Carlos Fuentes remembers, without the language of the colony there would not have been the language of independence. The Cuban, Argentinean, Uruguayan, Mexican, Spanish, and Paraguayan writers which up until this time have been honored with the Cervantes share the same language, with different literary accents enriched by the Hispanic multicultural reality. At the same time, and from different perspectives, they are parts of a common system in whose framework they institutionalize a literature.

Don Quijote and its author perform, and not in a rhetorical sense, the role of central character in this system. Alejo Carpentier recalls that as a child in his native city of Havana he played at the foot of a statue of don Miguel, which he considered to be the best ambassador that Spain ever had in his country through the course of the centuries; Jorge Luis Borges also realized this the very first time he read Don Quijote at the age of eight or nine, when he understood that the book's real hero was a knight touched by the passion of reading, or what Carlos Fuentes would call the madness of the manuscript. Some writers who have been honored with the prize that carries Cervantes' name such as Dámaso Alonso, Luis Rosales, Gonzalo Torrente Ballester, Carlos Fuentes and Francisco Ayala, have written reflexive and interpretive essays on the writer from Alcalá and his immortal novel.

Literature, understood as a system of functional relationships, finds this interchange of parts attractive: writers, having been first readers, are able to turn themselves into critics of what others have written, when not directly making recreations of the originals, as might have been the case with the version of Rafael Alberti's Numancia, directed by Margarita Xirgú in Montevideo; the short story by Borges titled "Pierre Menard, Author of Don Quijote", archetype of post-modern fiction; or the emotional "Parabola of Cervantes and of Quijote". The concept of literature I am proposing includes multiple perspectives that crisscross and necessarily have implications for each individual life and for the history of different peoples. We must take into account the position from which something is written and the position from which it is read, in both spatial and temporal, intellectual and institutional terms: For whom was it written, or for whom was it believed to be written, and to what extent has the writer's foresight anticipated the reality which has come to pass? It is important that we all understand what part of our literary tradition is shared and what part is foreign; we must ask ourselves which focuses of diffusion are central and which ones are peripheral, to what extent the editors are willing to believe in the value of a book and invest in its production and distribution, and what channels are available for coming to an agreement with such editors. Besides these issues, we must also consider the effects of political mediation and censorship, the influence of intellectual reflection on poetic creations, the power of literary criticism, the repertory of forms, styles, themes and visions of our universe that each community interprets in their own way, all and all, the horizon from which readers, both as individuals and as a collective, actually await and receive each new text. When at a given moment a high number of these factors, along with others that could have been mentioned, converge, and when their movement throughout a vast geographic community is free and active, as is the case in the Iberian Peninsula in Europe, and in the American Continent, then we may speak of a living literary system.

Jorge Guillén, who had taught at the Universidad de los Andes in Bogotá, received, (before accepting the first Cervantes Prize in 1977), the Alfonso Reyes Prize from Mexico. The first and failed attempt at writing sonnets undertaken by Gerardo Diego at the age of fourteen took as its inspiration Don Quijote, and his personal encounter in 1918 with the Chilean poet Vicente Huidobro opened his eyes to *creacionismo*. Borges was already aware of this movement through his coffee house conversations, before Diego traveled to Buenos Aires and Montevideo in 1928, and with him shared the Cervantes in 1979. Juan Carlos Onetti lived between these two cities in the Río de la Plata until his definitive move to Madrid in 1975. His first work appeared in Buenos Aires in newspapers such as La Nación, magazines like Sur, and publishing companies like Sudamérica or Compañía Fabril Editora. Meanwhile, the Uruguayan writer was publishing in the Montevideo periodical Marcha, but since Dejemos hablar al viento (1979) his work has been published in Spain, where Onetti identifies himself with the "thousands of the children of America that have found a new homeland in the homeland of Cervantes", as he emotionally manifested in his 1981 speech.

Mexico has had the same effect on many Spaniards exiled from the second Spanish Republic, such as the poets Emilio Prados, José Moreno Villa, Luis Cernuda, and León Felipe, who were cited and recited by Rafael Alberti in the central hall of Alcalá one day in April of 1984. Among the hundreds of their compatriots taken in by President Cárdenas was don Manuel Pedroso, former Rector of the University of Seville, who once taught a young Carlos Fuentes "the principles of the rights of peoples, non-intervention, autodetermination, peaceful solution to conflicts, coexistence of systems", as Fuentes himself remembered on a similar occasion. Fuentes' biography, encompasses the extraordinary possibilities offered by the Hispanic experience. Born in Panama, resident in Quito, Montevideo, Santiago de Chile and Buenos Aires, his work was already well known and appreciated when in 1967 he won the Biblioteca Breve Prize, the most important literary prize in Spain at the time, for his novel Cambio de piel that was, nevertheless, censored in Spain, while being printed in Mexico by Joaquín Mortiz. His novel Terra Nostra (1975), which he began to write immediately after Cambio de piel, is an impressive monument to the passionate conflict between Mexico and Spain, and obtained the Javier Villaurrutia Prize, and the Venezuelan Rómulo Gallegos Prize. Notification that he had received the Cervantes Prize reached Carlos Fuentes at the very moment that he was teaching a course at Harvard entitled "The tradition of La Mancha", concerned with looking at Don Quijote as a predecessor of the modern novel, the theme of one of his books of literary criticism, Cervantes o la crítica de la lectura from 1976. In another of his books, La nueva novela hispanoamericana (1972), he proposes Juan Goytisolo, along with Vargas Llosa, Carpentier, García Márquez and Cortázar, as representatives of the encounter of the Spanish novel with that written in Latin America, and concludes with a thesis that comes to ratify the plausibility of what I am proposing here: "the end of Latin American regionalism coincides with the end of European universalism: we are all in the middle to the extent that all of us are eccentric."

This same idea was central to the acceptance speech given by Dámaso Alonso, literary theorist and poet, upon receiving the Cervantes Prize, for whom, as well as for other Spanish poets, the impact produced by the Nicaraguan Rubén Darío was fundamental. A great part of Alonso's efforts as a linguist were dedicated to a principle which was precisely the title of one of his scholarly works: "We Spaniards are not masters of our language". The danger of fragmentation that hangs over a language shared by twenty nations on two continents, of approximately three hundred million speakers, has been conjured up, in a great part, by the existence of a common literary language irradiating from various centers, simultaneous or alternative, in accordance with changing historical conditions. Don Dámaso concludes by calling forth from the language the triumph of positive passions such as brotherhood and solidarity over nationalistic interests. But it is impossible to estimate the value, strictly in a literary sense, of this tension between the metropolitan center, and what Onetti calls, "the distant peripheries of the Spanish language". Octavio Paz in his acceptance speech reminds us, that for America and in America "Spain borders on the unknown": a statement which has a literal and symbolic meaning.

In modern times, Ramón del Valle-Inclán appears to be the writer most impacted by this perception. First, due to the fact that he belonged to a Spanish community in which the shared common language coexists with the vernacular, in this case Galician; secondly, due to his experiences as a youth in America that go back to 1892 which produced the writing of <u>Sonata de estío</u>, which was set in Mexico. Both substrates explain an extraordinarily free and creative attitude in the writer towards metropolitan language, leaning towards a universal "Castilian" rather than a provincial "Spanish". In contrast to those purist writers geographically and vitally anchored in their language, who spontaneously know by their intuition what to say clearly and distinctly and the rules they must never transgress, there are other writers who, from the peripheries of the predominant language, manipulate and distort it without ever getting to the point of causing its destruction, but on the contrary, endow it with creativity, as is the case of Ramón del Valle-Inclán and others. <u>Tirano Banderas</u>, a work known and admired by Miguel Angel Asturias, included in just one paragraph "American idioms from every land. . . from the "lepero to the gaucho style", as Valle-

Inclán revealed in a letter written in 1923 to the Mexican writer Alfonso Reyes.

Valle-Inclán's model of the "novela del dictador" was used in another Cervantine work, Yo el Supremo, by the Paraguayan Augusto Roa Bastos, which, due to the dictatorship that shackled his country, had to be published in Buenos Aires, as had also happened with Hijo del hombre, winner of the International award of the prestigious Losada publishing house, created by a Spaniard in 1938, after breaking with the Espasa-Calpe company which had sent him to South America to direct its business operations there. Gonzalo Losada, friend to his writers, understood that publishing houses were companies that produced culture, and from the beginning counted on the assistance of Spanish and Hispanic intellectuals such as Guillermo de Torre, Pedro Henríquez Ureña, Amado Alonso, the Hispano-Argentinian philosopher Francisco Romer, and the graphic artist Atilio Rossi. His role as mediator had a great impact, not only in creating an important publishing industry in Argentina, which later would extend to Peru, Chile, Colombia, and Uruguay, but which also, at the end of the Spanish Civil War and the subsequent cultural waste land, came to inherit the editorial hegemony of the Spanish language, and even to supply books to the Spaniards themselves.

Few documents offer a more complete and fascinating picture of this Latin American community of writers, artists, thinkers, critics, editors and readers, than the memoirs of the *granadino* Francisco Ayala, entitled Recuerdos y olvidos, who taught and published his famous studies in sociology in Buenos Aires, collaborated with La Nación and Victoria Ocampo's Sur, and participated in intellectual debates with her and with Borges, and founded the magazine Realidad, as he would later do again in Puerto Rico with La Torre. His novels Muertes de perro and El fondo del vaso, both of them originally published in Buenos Aires in 1958 and 1962 respectively, dealt with the realities of a dictatorship in an unnamed Central American Republic, of a calculated geographical ambiguity, much like the one that Gonzalo Torrente Ballester, author of a theatrical version of Lope de Aguirre in 1941, would use four years later in his novel El golpe de estado de Guadalupe Limón.

On the other hand, Alejo Carpentier's Ecue-Yamba-O, historia afrocubana, whose title comes from a Lucumi expression which means "God, how worthy of praise you are", was first published in Spain in 1933. Sixteen years later his second novel

El reino de este mundo was published in Mexico. The prologue was an authentic manifesto for the new Latin American novel, articulating his theory of the marvelous reality, "lo real maravilloso". In that prologue he claimed that what we call reality is a mentally and culturally socialized construction, which can change, and in fact does change, from one era to another. Carpentier recalls that in the middle of the 18th Century, while some intellectuals were fighting for the dissemination of the ideas of the Enlightment, "some reasonable Spaniards took off from Angostura" still looking for El Dorado, and the *Compostelan* Francisco Menéndez searched for the Enchanted City of the Caesars in Patagonia. What is most significant is that Carpentier is able to find a relationship between his own marvelous realism and the tradition that since Amadís de Gaula and Tirant lo Blanc leads to Don Quijote itself. For him, as it was for Cervantes in Chapter 47 of the first part of his immortal novel, the key is that the formal logic of writing is strictly maintained, even when the logic of the narrated world is subverted by the denaturalization of the real and the naturalization of the imagined, uniting "concocted fables with the understanding of those who read them".

Few literatures, such as those which have been tied to the Miguel de Cervantes Prize since 1976, can offer a system which is so stable and integrated in its relationship with factors such as tradition and renovation, writers and audiences, centers and peripheries, models and exceptions, creators and mediators, censorship and freedom, critics and readers. To speak, then, of a literature of two continents beyond a mere geographic definition makes perfect sense. This notion is supported by the diverse personalities and trajectories of those writers who have already received the prize, but also by those authors who have not yet been so honored, such as Nobel Prize winners Camilo José Cela and Gabriel Garcia Márquez.

Works cited

Even-Zohar,Itamar. "Polysystem Studies." Poetics Today. 11(1990): 1.

Schmidt, Siegfried J. Fundamentos de la ciencia empírica de la literatura. Madrid: Ediciones Taurus, 1990.

Villanueva, Darío, editor. Historia y crítica de la literatura española. Los nuevos nombres1975-1990. Barcelona: Editorial Crítica,1992.

## ¿Qué pueden los intelectuales?

Manuel Vázquez Montalbán y José Colmeiro

JC- José María Guelbenzu ha afirmado que la nueva función del intelectual es "dejar de proclamar la verdad para limitarse al esfuerzo de arrebatar una parte de ella a aquellos que traten de apoderarse de su totalidad". ¿Cúal es para Ud. el verdadero rol del intelectual en la cultura contemporánea?

MVM- La afirmación de Guelbenzu es como una reacción a una etapa en la que quizá el intelectual se ha caracterizado por hablar ex cátedra o dejar que los demás supongan que hablan ex cátedra. Yo creo que mientras exista una división del rol social, y en nuestra especialidad es manipular el lenguaje y a través del lenguaje influir y tratar de persuadir, por que en el fondo comunicar es persuadir, la influencia social del intelectual es real, pero no es tanta como la que pudiera haber tenido cuando el papel activo para los cambios sociales era muy de minorías y de élites y el mensaje de élite era un mensaje privilegiado. Ahora en una época en la que los mensajes son masivos, los sujetos históricos y sociales son masivos y la capacidad de alienarlos es extraordinaria como nunca lo había sido, hay que relativizar con una cierta humildad hasta donde puede llegar la pretensión de influencia social del intelectual. Luego matizar si es una parte de la verdad o si es toda la verdad, eso ya me parece que es un juego muy condicionado en algunos sectores por el miedo a haber hecho el ridículo durante demasiado tiempo proponiendo verdades demasiado absolutas y sistemáticas. Tampoco creo que desde este miedo o este pudor se pueda pasar a su contrario, a la abstención, a decir "ya que hemos hecho tanto el ridículo predibujando el mundo del futuro y profetizando, dejemos de predibujar y dejemos de profetizar".

JC- Una oposición importante entre dos maneras de situar la posición del intelectual sería la visión del intelectual como espectador de la cultura y otra como participante, como actor, dicotomía que ya planteaba en sus escritos subnormales, entre el intelectual como voyeur que "la sociedad utiliza como espectador de su propio cuerpo" (*Manifiesto subnormal*) y el intelectual como "actor del gran espectáculo de la insatisfacción" (*Cuestiones marxistas*).

MVM- Dos visiones bien decantadas que responden a la situación real. De los dos papeles prefiero el segundo porque a pesar de todas las ironías que puedas establecer, recibes al menos un mínimo de compensación ética y una cierta posibilidad de influencia, por decirlo así. Ya se que la vieja división entre el intelectual como reproductor de la ideología dominante y el intelectual que suministra la ideología de cambio es algo que habría que cuestionar muchísimo qué quiere decir y cómo se hace, pero que esas dos tendencias sobreviven y que se enmascaran ahora con mucha mayor sutileza y maquillajes más poderosos que hace unos años también es cierto. Ahora aparece todo un frente aparentemente muy audaz de una nueva vanguardia intelectual que predica precisamente la no ingerencia, el no mesianismo, pero en realidad su ingerencia y mesianismo es presentar un proyecto de sociedad único e inapelable, casi con unos mismos acentos totalitarios que pudiera haber adoptado un mensaje marxista y utópico en esa dirección hace 40 o 50 años.

JC- Una nota predominante en su escritura es la preeminancia de figuras de intelectuales heterodoxos y heterogeneos. Desde Carvalho a la galería de personajes de *Galíndez* o *El pianista* casi todos representan diferentes formas de asumir la intelectualidad: intelectuales comprados, vendidos, íntegros, mártires, light, de todos los tipos. ¿A qué responde esta constante interrogación por su parte sobre las mil caras del intelectual?

MVM- Es el prototipo humano que más me afecta por cuanto es al que más me parezco, es mi propio rol. Lógicamente es bastante probable que exista una obsesión a veces no del todo controlada por la investigación sobre la conducta de ese tipo de personajes en todas sus ramas: del triunfador al perdedor, el semi-triunfador, el semi-perdedor, el ético, el ético ambiguo, el ético absoluto, va apareciendo una variadísima rama. De hecho es una reflexión sobre mí mismo, no yo mismo encarnado como persona, sino como rol, como papel social, y todos esos personajes que has descrito podría haber sido yo cualquiera de ellos en una circunstancia determinada. Yo podría haber sido un Galíndez si hubiera vivido durante la Guerra Civil, o hubiera podido ser el pianista, u otro cualquiera de ellos, y si me hubieran ido mal las cosas hubiera podido ser el Marcial Pombo de la *Autobiografía del general Franco*. De hecho el personaje de Marcial Pombo, no exactamente el mismo, pero algún otro parecido, lo utilizo como miedo, como sombra del intelectual en *Los alegres muchachos de Atzavara*. Aparecía también otro personaje, el que no ha llegado a satisfacer las dosis de narcisismo que le proporciona el éxito literario. Aunque es cierto que eso forma parte de mi propia obsesión personal y seguro que ahí proyecto y sublimo problemas que no tengo del todo controlados.

JC- ¿Qué poder real de intervención tiene el intelectual en la sociedad aparte de su propia reflexión?

MVM- Hemos de dejar de auto-engañarnos en el sentido de pensar que nuestro rol es un rol determinante, un rol mesiánico derivado de aquella imaginería posromántica del intelectual poeta nacional conductor de pueblos, de masas o de vanguardias; eso sí que lo hemos de dejar completamente de lado porque no se corresponde en absoluto con la realidad. La consecuencia de eso sería abdicar del papel y pasar completamente a un papel pasivo de negación de influencia social y de intervención social, que no solamente sería una hipocresía sino una auténtica falacia porque el intelectual siempre interviene, en cualquier mensaje, y a poco cuerpo que tenga de una cierta bondad tanto ética como estética eso va a acabar influyendo, incluso por más abstencionista a priori que haya sido el intelectual. Hay una carga, le basta mirar y ofrecer una alternativa de mirada sobre la realidad para proponer de hecho una lectura del mundo, una alternativa a lo ya sabido o a lo ya contemplado si es un intelectual del pensamiento dedicado a repensar la realidad o si es un intelectual o un artista que se dedica a brindar una alternativa de la realidad mediante un código lingüístico. Solamente en la selección de esa mirada ya hay una concepción del mundo y una filosofía sobre los comportamientos, sobre las conductas, sobre el orden existente, por lo tanto hay una intervención ideológica y si no se aprecia contemporáneamente, con el tiempo si que se aprecia esa intervención ideológica. Reducir una lectura de cualquier propuesta literaria o intelectual a eso me parece una mezquindad, ahora prescindir de eso también me parecería una estupidez. No porque me parezca en un momento determinado Saint John Perse un poeta reaccionario por su visión del mundo, voy a dejar de pensar que es un excelente poeta, o el caso de T.S. Eliot, y en un mundo más complejo de novelistas del siglo XVII o XIX, cuya visión de la realidad nos puede parecer reaccionaria, pero que te los crees por verdades de caracter literario, no por verdades que provengan del terreno de la ideología.

JC- Sería el caso más contemporáneo de Borges. . .

MVM- Y sin embargo interviene ideológicamente. En Borges hay toda una visión del mundo de un evidente elitismo culterano.

JC- ¿De qué manera la escritura puede servir para combatir con la realidad?

MVM- La palabra combatir me parece excesiva. Pero la subjetivación de que la realidad no es suficiente en sí misma la puedes convertir en algo más global y universal propuesto a los demás. De hecho la realidad es el resultado de una manera de ordenar el caos, casi un principio filosófico, y deja muy contenta a la gente normal y corriente. Lo que más les molesta es que alguien les pueda decir "eso que Ud. cree que es un orden no es un orden", ya desde el punto de vista económico, vivencial, cotidiano, en las relaciones personales, la relación con el perro, con el hijo. Cuando el escritor trata de demostrar el caos que se esconde detrás del desorden está cuestionando la realidad que la gente tiene asumida, y lo que empieza siendo algo evidente para una persona, la magia consiste en que lo pueda hacer evidente para 2.000, 5.000 o 20,000 personas.

JC- Tras los fastos celebratorios de encuentros y desencuentros, Latinoamérica sigue siendo nuestro Sur histórico en el subconsciente colectivo. ¿Ha sido el año 92 la gran ocasión perdida para un verdadero encuentro de culturas? ¿Es más abundante la mala conciencia o la falta de conciencia?

MVM- Es como tú dices, la gran ocasión perdida, porque es el año que coge a España en plena democracia, con además un gobierno de izquierda, con toda la contradicción que significa para un gobierno de izquierda celebrar un hecho imperialista. Pero una vez asumido eso, los hechos son los hechos, era la gran ocasión de haber convertido eso en lo que pudo ser la sombra de las dos Conferencias Iberoamericanas, la de México y la de Madrid. Ese era el camino, preguntarnos dónde estamos, de dónde venimos ya lo sabemos, el mestizaje es un hecho que tenemos que asumir, en qué relaciones de dependencia y con qué poderes reales, qué condiciona que seamos Sur, qué quiere decir la deuda externa. Esa era la gran ocasión para situar el problema en sus justos términos actuales. Pero eso significaba encontrar víctimas y verdugos en esa relación, y ya no eran Hernán Cortés y Moctezuma; hoy las víctimas y verdugos tienen otros nombres y eso implicaba un problema muy serio de clarificación de la realidad. Lo que se ha producido como efecto más beneficioso es que se ha removido el poso de esta cuestión, ha servido para que nazca un movimiento indigenista de concienciación, o al menos que se haya activado muchísimo y se haya hablado mucho más de él desde Europa; el premio Nobel a Rigoberta Menchú no se lo hubieran dado sino hubiera sido por el 92. En cambio el que ha seguido mixtificando el asunto es el criollo. El criollo es el que sigue falsificando esa historia, porque sigue prefiriendo que el cabrón sea el español, que lo ha sido evidentemente, y olvide su propio cabronaje de 200 años durante los que ha practicado en los lugares donde estaba en posición hegemónica un exterminio tremendo de la población indígena. O sea que sí se ha desaprovechado el 92. Ha tenido unos efectos secundarios positivos, una cierta reflexión, pero el propio poder cultural y político español no ha sabido ni ponerle nombre; es que aún no sabemos qué ha sido, si un descubrimiento, si un encuentro, si un choque de culturas. . . no se sabe, porque ninguna familia ideológica se ha atrevido todavía a colocarle un nombre fijo.

Esta entrevista se realizó en Barcelona en diciembre de 1992 gracias a la ayuda del Programa de Estudios "Joan Maragall" de la Fundación José Ortega.

## Contributors

**Dionisio Cañas** (Tomelloso, 1949) has been living in New York since 1973, where he is a Professor at the City University of New York. He has published six poetry books, the last two being El fin de las razas felices (Hiperión, Madrid, 1987) y En lugar del amor (BAM, Diputación de Ciudad Real, 1990). He has published numerous studies on Spanish and Latin American poetry, among them the critical edition of José Hierro's Libro de las alucinaciones (1986) and Gil de Biedma's anthology, Volver (1989) both of them in Cátedra, as well as two works of literary criticism, Poesía y percepción (Hiperión, Madrid, 1984) and El poeta y la ciudad. Nueva York y los escritores hispanos (Cátedra, Madrid, 1994).

**José F. Colmeiro** (Vigo, 1958). Ph.D. in Hispanic Languages and Literatures (University of California, Berkeley). Associate Professor of Spanish at Dartmouth College. He has published numerous articles on Spanish fiction and film, and is the author of La novela policiaca española: Teoría e historia crítica (Anthropos, 1994) and Crónica del desencanto: La narrativa de Manuel Vázquez Montalbán (Univ. of Miami, North-South Center, 1996), awarded the "Letras de Oro" prize for best book-length essay in 1995.

**Marvin D'Lugo** is Professor of Spanish and director of Screen Studies at Clark University. He has written extensively on Spanish and Latin American cinemas. D'Lugo is the author of The Films of Carlos Saura: The Practice of Seeing (Princeton University Press, 1991), and he is currently completing a book-length study of theories of national cinema for Routledge Press.

**Christina Dupláa** (Barcelona, 1954). Ph. D. in Hispanic and Luso-Brazilian Literatures (University of Minnesota). "Licenciaturas" in Journalism and History, and MA in Spanish and Portuguese. Currently, Assistant Professor of Spanish at Dartmouth College. She has co-edited Las nacionalidades del Estado español: una problemática cultural and has published articles on the metaphorical role of the feminine figure in turn-of-the-century Catalonian nationalist discourse. At the present moment, she is preparing a book-length study on "La voz testimonial en Montserrat Roig".

**Cristina Enríquez de Salamanca** received her MA in 1990 and her Ph.D. in Spanish Literature from the University of Minnesota, Minneapolis in 1995. Co-author of Double Minorities of Spain. A Bio-Bibliographic Guide to Women Writers of the Catalan, Galician and Basque Countries and is on the Editorial Board of the *Biblioteca de Escritoras Españolas*. She has also published articles on nineteenth-century Peninsular literature and culture, Golden Age and Latin-American authors. She is a Visiting Assistant Professor of Spanish Literature at Yale University (1995-1996).

**Víctor Fuentes** was born in Madrid. He is Professor of 19th and 20th century Spanish Literature at the University of California, Santa Barbara. He has published numerous studies on literary history and criticism, cinema and the relationship between film and literature. His publications include La marcha del pueblo en las letras españolas: 1917-1936, El cántico material y espiritual de César Vallejo, Benjamín Jarnés: Bio-Grafía y Metaficción, and Buñuel en México.

**Patricia V. Greene** (Madrid 1958). Ph.D. in Hispanic Languages and Literatures (University of California, Berkeley). Visiting Assistant Professor of Spanish at Dartmouth College. She has published numerous articles on women's autobiographical practices in contemporary Spain and is guest Co-editor of *Duoda* "Mujeres y Literatura de Resistencia" (April 1996). Currently, she is preparing the book-length study "Constancia de la Mora: Confessions of a Communist Aristocrat".

**David K. Herzberger** is Professor of Spanish and Comparative Literature at the University of Connecticut. He is the author of books on Juan Benet (1976) and Jesús Fernández Santos (1983) and of Narrating the Past: Fiction and Historiography in Postwar Spain (1995). He has published numerous articles on modern Spanish literature in journals such as PMLA, Hispanic Review, Insula, MLN, Letras Peninsulares, and Journal of Aesthetics and Art Criticism. In 1991 he was awarded the William Riley Parker Prize by the Modern Language Association for his Study of Francoist historiography and the novel of memory.

**Susan Kirkpatrick** is Professor of Spanish Literature at the University of California, San Diego, where she is also director of Women's Studies. She is the author of Larra: El laberinto inextricable de un liberal romántico (1977) and Las románticas: Women Writers and Subjectivity in Spain, 1835-1850 (1989), and is editor of Antología Poética de Escritoras del Siglo XIX (1992). Currently she is investigating configurations of gender in Spain at the turn of the nineteenth century.

**Jaume Martí-Olivella** holds degrees in English Philology and Catalan Literature from the University of Barcelona and in Comparative Literature from the University of Illinois. He is a founding member of NACS (North American Catalan Society). Currently an associate professor of Spanish at Allegheny College, Martí-Olivella has published extensively on Peninsular film and fiction and on literary theory. He has edited two special issues of Catalan Review: "Homage to Merce Rodoreda" (Barcelona, 1987) and "Women, History and Nation in the Fiction of Maria Aurelia Capmany and Montserrat Roig" (Barcelona, 1993). He is also co-organizer of CINE-LIT I and II (First and Second International Conference on Hispanic Film and Fiction, Portland, 1991 and 1994). He is now at work on a book-length study on Spanish Cinema in the Classroom.

**Geraldine Nichols** is Professor of Spanish and Chair of the Department of Romance Languages and Literatures at the University of Florida. She received her M.A. and Ph.D. from the Johns Hopkins University, and has published extensively on Spanish Literature of the twentieth century. Her most recent books --Escribir, espacio propio: Laforet, Matute, Tusquets, Moix, Roig y Riera por sí mismas (Minneapolis: Institute for the Study of Ideologies and Literature, 1989), and Des/cifrar la diferencia: narrativa femenina de la España contemporánea (Madrid, Siglo XXI, 1991)-- deal exclusively with contemporary Catalonian women's fiction.

**Lourdes Ortiz**, Madrid, 1943, holds a degree in History from the Universidad Complutense de Madrid. She is currently Professor of Art History at the Real Escuela Superior de Arte Dramático de Madrid. Her numerous publications include her novels: Luz de la memoria, Picadura mortal, En días como estos..., Urraca, Arcángeles, Los motivos de Circe, and Antes de la batalla. Her essays about a variety of topics include Comunicación crítica, Rimbaud, Larra. Escritos políticos and Camas. She has translated into Spanish books by Flaubert, the Marquis de Sade, Bataille, Michel Tournier and Charles LeGoff's. She has published two children's short story books and one drama, and she has staged eight others. She is an active presence in Spanish newspapers and magazines, with political and cultural essays (El Mundo, Diario 16).

**Juana Sabadell Nieto** is Assistant Professor of Contemporary Spanish Literature at Dartmouth College. She received her Ph.D. and M.A. from the University of Pennsylvania and her Licenciatura in Ciencias de la Información from the Universidad de Navarra. Her book La palabra como existencia. Estudio sobre la poesía de Jaime Gil de Biedma is forthcoming in Winter 1996, in Prensa y Publicaciones Universitarias of the University of Barcelona. She has published articles in Spain and the United States on English and Spanish Poetry, on the definition of poetic "genres", on problems of subjectivity, and on Gil de Biedma and other poets. Currently she is working on a book-length project that will study the gender relations and the linguistic boundaries that define the multi-cultural literature of contemporary Spain, analyzing recent poetry produced in the country's four languages by both men and women writers.

**Paul Julian Smith** is Professor and Head of the Department of Spanish and Portuguese at the University of Cambridge. His books include The Body Hispanic: Gender and Sexuality in Spanish and Spanish American Literature (Oxford: Oxford University Press, 1989), Representing the Other: 'Race', Text and Gender in Spanish and Spanish American Narrative (Oxford: Oxford University Press, 1992), Laws of Desire: Questions of Homosexuality in Spanish Writing and Film 1960-90 (Oxford: Oxford University Press, 1992), Desire Unlimited: The Cinema of Pedro Almodóvar (London : Verso, 1994), ¿Entiendes? Queer Readings/Hispanic Texts (Durham: Duke University Press, 1995). Forthcoming 1996 Vision Machines (London: Verso).

**Darío Villanueva** (1950) is currently the President of the Universidade de Santiago de Compostela and also holds the chair of Literary Theory. He has been a visiting professor or invited lecturer at various Universities in Argentina, Belgium, Canada, the United States, France, The Netherlands, Portugal, Great Britain, and Switzerland. He has published more than fifty articles on theory, criticism, and comparative literature. His most recent books are El comentario de textos narrativos, la novela (1989, 1992), El polen de las ideas (1991), Trayectoria de la novela hispanoamericana actual (1991), of which he is co-author with J.M. Viña Liste, and Teorías del realismo literario (1992), finalist for Spain's Premio Nacional de Ensayo in 1993 and currently being translated into English by the State University of New York Press.